MW01241176

"Combining her a
unfailing eye for t
tapestry of ordinary events and episodes that bring out the
extraordinary nature of life in a foreign land. Arriving in the US
with Hollywood-generated constructs, ideas and impressions that
have rendered her unprepared for the culture shock awaiting her,
the author freely allows her perceptive mind to experience the
novelties and frailties around her.

"Added to interesting titbits are the author's highly
insightful comments on the social, cultural and linguistic quirks
of American life. The result is an absorbing narrative that is at
once devilishly satirical and delightfully humorous."

*— **Professor B. Kumaravadivelu***
Professor of Applied Linguistics
San Jose State University, California, USA

"Scintillating! A unique eye-opening and hearty discourse on
the experiences of a Nyonya in the la-la land of the bighorn,
scribed in a very readable earthy style! Funny, provocative and
useful as a travelogue as well as an academic treatise for students
of cross-culturalism anywhere."

*— **Mano Maniam***
Malaysian Theatre Practitioner, Fulbright Scholar

"She juggles the serious and the funny, sometimes making our
laughter catch in our throats and sometimes making us smile
even when we want to sigh. Her tales gain deeper dimensions
from the fact that she speaks both as a member of a diminishing
minority in a small country in a globalised world, and as a carrier
of ancient cultures at the same time."

*— **Ooi Kee Beng, PhD***
Fellow, Institute of Southeast Asian Studies, Singapore

"As a Chinese national raised in China and speaking English as a second language, I have lived in the US for more than eight years. As a result of this, I have experienced on a firsthand basis what Lee Su Kim has written about."

— *Yunfang Wendy Guo, Partner*
China Tax and Business Advisory Services
PricewaterhouseCoopers, Beijing, China

"Each story exposes the habits, myths, misconceptions and expectations of everyone in every conversation which takes place. Every story is a lesson in humanity. A witty and comical exposé. A must for everyone who wants to appreciate American culture and habits."

— *Dr Lawrence Freeman*
President and Chief Executive Officer
Global Business Consultants Inc, USA

"A light and insightful page turner that vividly captures the obvious and subtle differences of Asian and American culture. A **must read** for anyone who is interested in understanding cultural differences—Asians, new immigrants and Americans alike!"

— *Lili Zheng*
International Tax Partner (Deloitte Tax LLP)
Deputy Managing Partner (Chinese Services Group, USA)

"Initially, I thought that this book would sensitise me to how immigrants feel coming to the US. It did but it does so much more. It builds awareness of some American habits and tendencies that certainly have room for improvement. This kind of enlightenment makes it a must read for all."

— *Professor Lloyd Shefsky*
(Clinical) Professor of Entrepreneurship
Northwestern University's Kellogg School of Management and
author of the acclaimed Entrepreneurs are Made Not Born

a Nyonya in TEXAS

Insights of a Straits Chinese Woman in the Lone Star State

To Janet,
With Best Wishes,

Lee Su Kim
31 July 2010

LEE SU KIM

Marshall Cavendish
Editions

© 2007 Text by Lee Su Kim
© 2007 Marshall Cavendish (Malaysia) Sdn Bhd
(General & Reference Publishing)

Illustrations by Muhamad Azhar Abdullah

Published by Marshall Cavendish Editions
An imprint of Marshall Cavendish International

Other Marshall Cavendish Offices:
Marshall Cavendish Ltd. 119 Wardour Street, London W1F 0UW • Marshall Cavendish Corporation. 99 White Plains Road, Tarrytown NY 10591-9001 • Marshall Cavendish International (Thailand) Co Ltd. 253 Asoke, 12th Flr, Sukhumvit 21 Road, Klongtoey Nua, Wattana, Bangkok 10110, Thailand • Marshall Cavendish International (Asia) Private Limited. Times Centre, 1 New Industrial Road, Singapore 536196

Marshall Cavendish is a trademark of Times Publishing Limited

National Library Board (Malaysia) Cataloguing in Publication Data

Lee Su Kim
    A nyonya in Texas : insights of a straits Chinese woman in the
    Lone star state / Lee Su Kim.
    ISBN 978-983-3346-10-3
    ISBN 983-3346-10-3
    1. Lee, Su Kim--Anecdotes. 2. Expatriation--Texas--Anecdotes.
    3. Peranakan--Anecdotes. I. Title.
    305.9069109764

Printed in Malaysia by Times Offset (Malaysia) Sdn Bhd

To my son Lee Jan Ming

Acknowledgements

I would like to thank my many friends in the United States of America, Malaysia and all around the world who have encouraged me to write this book. I am indebted to two wonderful professors in the US, who touched my life and were a bastion of strength and support, Professor Phil Francis Carspecken and the late Professor Henry Trueba. Thank you to all the great friends I made in the US—to Jeannie Kim, Lilian Foo, Valentina Hardin, Sugar Martinez, Anne Brown, Ruth Silva, Sim Chandler, Phaik See Lim, Keith James, Sabrina Walton, and to many more who made my sojourn in the US such a memorable one. To Carlton and Marilyn Johnson, I am grateful to you both for the love and hospitality you showered on my family. To the people who stood by us when the going got rough, friends at Exxon and EPMI, and old school friends from the VI, BBGS and MU, my heartfelt gratitude. To the many Americans I met who encouraged me to write this book even though I told them it was going to take the mickey out of them, I am delighted at your wonderful sense of humour and generosity of spirit. I do hope I can still get through US immigration if I should visit the US.

I would like to thank Universiti Kebangsaan Malaysia for

allowing me the opportunity to pursue my doctorate in the US. As always, my thanks to a dear friend, Harriet Wong whose enthusiasm and magnanimity never cease to amaze me. My thanks go to my uncles, Foo Yat Kee and Yat Chin for regaling me with their wonderful stories and inspiring me with their infectious love of life. To Patricia Lee, and to my sister Su Win and brother Yu Ban, thank you. To the many friends, colleagues, teachers, academics and others who keep asking me, "When is your next book?"—my thanks to all of you for being such an inspiring force.

I would like to thank Dato' Steven Tan (Managing Director), Dato' Ng Poh Tip (Group Editorial and Education Adviser and Executive Director of the Asian Centre for Media Studies), and the people at *The Star*; as well as Dato' Ng Tieh Chuan (Chief Executive Officer of MPH Group Publishing) and Eric Forbes of Pelanduk Publications for their support in my writing career.

I am deeply indebted to Stephen Hall for his encouragement, his love and support. Without him, this book may never have gotten off the ground. I am also grateful to him for his helpful comments, editing skills, and his belief in my work. To Nancy Hall, thank you for your kindness and wisdom. I would like to thank a dear friend, Alan Maley for reading through the manuscript and for his interest in this book. My thanks also go to the great team at Marshall Cavendish (M) Sdn Bhd, particularly to Christine Chong (Deputy Head) and my excellent editor, Manjula Aryaduray.

Finally, my thanks to my son, Jan Ming, who took a personal interest in the book and read every essay. The expressions on his face, his smiles, his frowns and his comments helped me to craft complexity with clarity in each essay, and relive those special, significant and quirky moments of our sojourn in Texas.

Preface

I am a Nyonya. I belong to the Peranakan community, a unique ethnic group which evolved a long time ago in Old Malacca on the west coast of Malaysia. The Peranakan means 'locally born' in Malay. We are also known as Straits Chinese, with the terms Babas for the males and Nyonyas for the females. This community evolved in the fifteenth century when traders from China arrived in Malacca and married local women. The Peranakan culture is a rare and beautiful blend of two cultures—Malay and Chinese—in a fascinating synthesis with elements of Javanese, Batak, Siamese, British and Portuguese cultures. We were, and continue to be, the epitome of 'multiculturalism' and 'fusion' long before the terms were invented.

In 1996, I went to live in Texas, USA, and stayed there for more than three years. I lived there in many capacities—a postgraduate student pursuing a doctoral degree, an expatriate wife, a mother, a homemaker, a writer, and a university don on study leave. Just as foreigners visit 'exotic' countries and cultures in the East and document them, I realised the reverse was also necessary. As an outsider, a woman writer from Asia, now living as an insider in the US, I encountered many fascinating and unique cultural differences as well as similarities between two peoples living on opposite sides of the world. Some of the articles were written while living in Texas and some after my return home to Malaysia.

Here is my story of a Nyonya in Texas.

Contents

Paper or Plastic?

My stay of more than three years in Houston, Texas kicked off with the most mundane of tasks. As my family and I had been relocated there, we needed to purchase a number of boring ordinary things vital for the smooth functioning of a household. The supermarket was enormous—I had never been to something quite as huge as this. The aisles were wide enough for a golf cart to drive through, and the shelves were stocked with every conceivable product under the sun. Initially, it was smooth sailing for me. Shopping was after all a universal pastime, no matter what one's colour, culture or nationality. It was only when I reached the checkout counter that my problems began.

First of all, I was startled by the absolute cheerfulness and friendliness of the staff. Back in my home country, transactions at the supermarkets or hypermarkets are a totally non-verbal affair. The checkout girls do not smile or greet or thank you, they mechanically reach out for the stuff you put in front of them, scan them, and accept your payment—all without a single word exchanged between payer and payee.

Here in this sleek gleaming American supermarket, the staff members were, horror of horrors, very friendly.

The sales assistant at the checkout counter greeted me cheerfully, "Good Morning, Mam! How ya doin'?"

"Good morning," I mumbled, "I'm er … doin' very well, thank you."

This was quite similar to the greetings back home such as the Malay greeting, '*Apa khabar?*' (What's the news?) to which you usually respond '*Khabar baik*' (The news is good). Even if you are being chased by the Income Tax Department or have received seven summonses for traffic offences, or are having a bad hair day, the normal way to respond is to say that 'The news is good'. Likewise, the Chinese in Malaysia have a greeting 'Have you eaten?' when they meet you, to which you respond 'Yes, I have. How about you?' Of course, no one is interested in your latest trendy diet or that you have just gobbled a bowl of the most divine *assam laksa* (a spicy fish-based noodle soup), or lobsters sautéed in a fragrant sauce of white asparagus, lemon grass and julienned mushrooms washed down with the most amazing Pinot Noir … no need to go into details, just a simple response will do as it is just a greeting.

It was the second question the checkout lady asked that stumped me.

"Paper or Plastic, Mam?" she wanted to know in a strong nasal drawl.

Paper? Plastic? How strange … what on earth did she mean by it?

If she had said 'Paper, Scissors, Stone' I might have fared better, but 'Paper or Plastic?' couldn't quite gel in my jet-lagged brain at that moment.

Aha, got it! That's it! I whisked out my most favourite piece of plastic in the world—all eight by five centimetres of it and handed it to her with a flourish.

"Do you accept Visa?" I asked. "It ain't American Express but I never leave home without it." I smiled and winked at her.

She didn't seem terribly charmed. In fact, she seemed to be getting impatient by the minute and was entering decidedly decibel-raising territory, "PAPER OR PLASTIC, MAM? AH AIN'T GOT ALL DAY."

I cringed with horror. Arrggh, tone down your voice, Woman, Ah ain't deaf, Ah thought.

I was getting impatient and irritated too—not at her but at myself. After all, I had spent a lifetime watching American movies churned out from Hollywood. American movies were a far better orientation course than sitting through a formal lecture on 'Starting Out In Your New Life in America' in some confined lecture room.

Hasta la Vista, Baby … Go Ahead Make My Day … You Complete Me … Show Me the Money! … Love Means Never Having to Say You're Sorry … Frankly My Dear, I Don't Give a Damn … As God is My Witness, I'll Never Be Hungry Again … Me Tarzan, You Jane … I'm the King of the World … I Want to be Left Alone … May the Force be with You … ET Phone Home … Houston, We Have a Problem …

All those famous quotes from the movies still swimming in my head, but 'Paper or Plastic?' I had never come across that one … !

Then, from the corner of my eye, I saw a pile of paper bags and plastic bags on the checkout counter.

"PLASTIC!" I snapped.

Everything worked like clockwork after that. She checked out my purchases, packed my stuff into plastic bags and I happily wheeled them away to my car. Here in Texas, one is given a choice between paper or plastic—the customer can make a stand for the environment and choose paper, which is recyclable, over plastic, which isn't. Back home at the supermarkets, one's purchases are packed away into plastic and more plastic, never mind what your environmental sympathies are.

The next stop was a fast-food restaurant. I placed my order at the counter, and was asked another unfamiliar question of the day.

"For Here or To Go, Mam?" the cashier asked me.

"Huh? Go … er … go where?" I asked.

"Ah dunno! How am Ah suppos' to know where yer' goin', Girl?" the cashier growled at me.

It's tough to be regarded as an idiot when you're positively sure you're not. But that must have been how I must have looked to him.

Then, a brilliant stroke of genius hit me.

"Oh, you mean Takeaway! Oh, okay, I am having it Here … not to go … er … I mean I'm not going anywhere. Oh, never mind," I muttered.

Jeepers Creepers or is it Holy Moly, but I thought the whole English-speaking world used the phrase 'Takeaway'. How come no one ever told me Americans speak funny English? 'For Here or To Go?' sounded grammatically incorrect to me. Whatever happened to good trustworthy nouns or the versatile gerunds of the English language?

What took place next gave an even bigger jolt to my system. Instead of I not being able to understand the Texans, this time they couldn't understand me. This really rattled me as I thought I was using my most impeccable English. At the Texas Department of Public Safety, I was trying to get my American driving licence as soon as possible. A driving licence here is very important and serves almost as an identity card. I needed to fix an appointment to do the test. After waiting for hours in the queue, it was my turn to speak to the officer at the counter. The Asian-American lady asked me, "When do you want to take your test?"

I purred politely in elegant immaculate English … or so I thought, "I wonder if it would be possible for me to take my driving test next Tuesday?"

She looked at me blankly. She couldn't understand me and repeated her question. This was nerve-wracking. I tried again, this time with less embedded clauses.

"If it is okay with you, could I take the test next Tuesday?" I posed my question to her.

She was getting irritated. She looked as though she was hyper-ventilating. She snapped, "Mam, when do you want to take the test?"

Oh, oh, I am getting nowhere here. Help, I need that blasted driving licence. She is not impressed with my good/ bad English. She must be the kind who hates questions being answered with questions.

Quick, no time to lose, ditch your hoity-toity English and speak direct-in-your-face American English. My American friends did warn me that one has got to be very direct and assertive here in the US. I raised my voice ten decibels louder, stuck my thumbs into my Levi's jeans, did a John Wayne swagger, and demanded my rights, "I WANT TO TAKE IT NEXT TUESDAY."

The officer said, "Okay. Next Tuesday at 11 A.M."

I was stunned. It worked. I forgot and lapsed into gentle polite mode again.

"Er … What do I have to bring along with me next Tuesday?" I asked.

She replied curtly, "You just bring yourself."

I was stumped by this. Back home, no one of sane mind ever goes to a government department to apply for something, empty-handed. That would be suicidal. Usually you arm yourself with all the certificates, photographs and documents you can muster, plus a copier machine if that were only possible, so that you will be spared the ultimate torture—the dreaded eternal run-around. All you need is to tangle with one officious bureaucrat who likes to practise a slow wilting torture by making you return over and over again because of one missing document or another. Was she being sarcastic? How could I just possibly bring myself and nothing else? That was like opting for sheer nudity.

Anyway, come next Tuesday, I just 'brought myself', did the test and wonder of wonders, got the licence!

Polar Opposites

When you first arrive in the US, it sure is hard to spend your money. If you don't have some vital numbers to your name, you don't count in the scheme of things. This thing called a credit history was a real puzzler. During my first week in Houston, I tried to buy a grandfather clock at a huge furniture store. The attraction was that you could take the clock home with you and pay up next year, interest-free. I found that quite an irresistible marketing strategy or was it the grandfather clock that I found irresistible? Anyway, the problems started when I got to the cashier.

"What's your Social Security Number?" she asked.

"Er … I don't have any Social Security. What's that? I have just arrived in the US."

"What's your Driving License Number?" she queried.

"I haven't taken my driving test yet. I'm new here in the US. I arrived a few days ago," I responded.

She seemed determined to extract some kind of number from me. I tried to help, "How about my IC number? My Identity Card number from my country?"

She said, "No, that won't do. Do you have a credit history?"

"No, I don't owe anyone credit," I replied with some measure of pride, confident that this would certainly impress the lady on what a good paymaster I was.

She stared at me as if she couldn't believe that I did not owe any money. For someone who wanted to buy a noisy, ticking grandfather clock on arrival in a new country, I must have raked up a fortune buying equally vital and necessary objects, I am sure she thought that of me.

I continued, "It's true. I do not owe anyone any money. 'If you can't afford it, then you don't need it' is my motto."

Meanwhile, the grandfather clock continued tick-tocking away merrily at the corner of the vast floor. It brought back powerful memories of my grandpa and my mother, who loved to sing the old folksong 'My Grandfather's Clock' to us as children.

My Grandfather's Clock was too large for the shelf
So it stood ninety years on the floor …
Ninety years without slumbering tick tock tick tock
His life's seconds numbering tick tock tick tock
But it stopped short never to go again
When the old man died.

"Then you don't qualify. No credit history," the woman pronounced.

"What? But how can I have a history when I haven't even got a past? I've only been here a few days!" I protested.

It was the same the whole week long—really hard to buy anything because one had not raked up anything on credit. It was a matter of pride not to owe money in my culture, even buying something on an instalment basis was considered rather embarrassing. On the contrary, here in the US, I learnt that if you don't have a credit history, then it is embarrassing—you have no potential as someone who can be trusted to pay on credit, and therefore cannot be trusted.

More interesting contradictions awaited me the longer my sojourn here in the Lone Star State.

Driving on the Wrong Side of the Road

Americans drive on the wrong side of the road. Or should I say, they drive on the right side of the road whereas we Malaysians drive on the left side, following the British system. I can understand if the Romans or the Greeks chose to differ but I wonder who it was who decided to dump the British system and chose to cross over to the other side. Perhaps having to fight for Independence from the Pommies had something to do with it, but then other previous 'British colonies' such as India, Sri Lanka, Brunei, Malaysia and Singapore still faithfully cling to the left side of the road, long after the Brits left the scene.

It was quite a problem adjusting to this. No matter how hard I tried to internalise this piece of culture shock, it would occasionally slip my mind. Whenever I tried to cross the road, I would look to my right and finding the road absolutely clear, make a cross over, and end up almost getting killed, as the traffic was coming the other way! Even after living in Texas for more than a year, when about to drive somewhere, I would walk to the right side of my car (which is wrong in the US as the driver's side is on the left side of the car) and suffer from shock attacks wondering where my steering wheel had gone to!

Still Imperial

When my country, and I assume the rest of the world, switched over to the metric system, I was rather sad to see the old Imperial system go. I had been educated in the British Imperial system and was used to buying and counting eggs in dozens, weighing flour and butter in pounds and ounces, milk and liquids in pints and gallons. I measured length and depth in feet and inches, distances in miles, and bought materials in yards. At the wet market, I bought fish, chicken or onions in *katis* and *tahil*. I loved the words of the Imperial system—pound, ounce, inch, yard, acre, *gantang*, peck, pint, bushel, barrel, furlong, fathom, league, Fahrenheit. It was hard to fathom why the world wanted to change to the metric system when the Imperial one was such a barrel of fun. I resisted for a long time—for me, Shylock would always insist on his pound of flesh, one dozen red roses would always mean I love you, and Peter Pecker would always pick his peck of pepper.

However, as the world became metricated, I too had to change and operate in the metric system. I had to face the truth—the metric system where units of measurement are a number of impersonal zeroes, may be cold and functional, but it is much more efficient and helps ensure standardisation throughout the world.

With time, I eventually mastered the metric system. Although my height will always be in feet and inches and my weight in pounds, as I haven't gotten around to converting them, in everything else, I operate in metric units. Imagine my immense surprise then when I came to the US and could not be understood when I spoke in metric and not Imperial!

"Can I have five hundred grammes of the prawns, please?" I politely place an order at the seafood section of the American supermarket.

"Huhh?? Can I help you, Mam?" the sales assistant at the counter asks me.

"Er … oops I mean err … let me see … half a pound of the prawns err … I mean shrimps … err I mean *heaffapouun* of the shrimps, please? Thank you," I reply.

Not only do I have to sort out the varieties of English—British English and American English, and the different ways of pronunciation, I have had to reconvert back to the old Imperial system. How incredible to think that the Americans have sent astronauts to outer space but they have still not converted to the metric system. After all, it is, as the first man on the moon would put it, just "one small step" for mankind.

Staying True

My ancestors ain't gonna be very happy about this ... I just know it ... My forefathers will frown if they but knew about this. For here in the US, after just six months I have caved in to American might and committed a terrible sin. I have blatantly, oh so brashly, relocated my surname—the all important portion of a Chinese name—from first name to last name and last position.

I belong to an ethnic group in Malaysia which is a unique synthesis of two cultures. The Straits Chinese or Peranakan culture, as it is called, evolved as far back as the fifteenth century when traders from China settled in Malacca, and married the local Malay women there. Gradually, a new culture evolved which is Chinese in form but Malay in substance. Names, societal structure, religious practices and rites and rituals are Chinese but language, cuisine and dress are Malay in essence.

I grew up in a world where Malay and Chinese cultural elements, as well as a sprinkling of English, European, Javanese and Siamese elements interwove itself into a fascinating tapestry. Food was a wonderful blend of Chinese and Malay with lots of spicy curries and *sambals*, and a variety of herbs and spices. On special occasions, Grandmother and Mother wore beautiful *kebayas*, a local traditional costume comprising of flimsy Swiss voile tops, delicately embroidered with motifs of flowers and birds, matched with colourful batik *sarongs* from Java, Indonesia. The music of the Babas and Nyonyas was Malay in influence while many rituals were Chinese in origin. Grandpa and Grandma spoke to my siblings and I in Baba Malay—a Malay patois with many words of Hokkien, English and Portuguese origin—while my parents spoke English and Hokkien to us. I learnt Cantonese, a Chinese dialect, from our amah, our live-in nanny.

While the essence of the Peranakan culture is Malay, the form is Chinese and therefore the Chinese name is all important. Yet after half a year in the US, one would think that I could at least stay intact but no, I have tinkered around with my name, contorted it, in fact—something which a Chinese would never do in China, Taiwan, Hong Kong nor Southeast Asia.

"Stay true to yourself," a friend had advised me before I left for the US.

"What do you mean?" I asked puzzled.

"Stay in touch with your inner being, enjoy the new experiences, adapt to your new life but do not change the essence of who you are," he said.

Who me, change? Naahh, I don't think so. I wasn't exactly in my formative years anymore, and I happen to be proud of my Malaysian identity and cultural heritage. I wasn't a likely candidate for change at all. Although I had travelled to various parts of the world, I qualify as a true 'home-grown' product. I was educated at a local school and received my tertiary education from the University of Malaya. I had never experienced living in a foreign country, except for holidays abroad.

And now I was off to the US to pursue a postgraduate

degree as well as to accompany my husband on an international assignment. My whole family was about to be relocated to Houston, Texas. A secret dream—the opportunity to study abroad—was about to materialise. I would treasure the experience and eventually return, nothing would change, I would always still be me.

I was in for a big surprise. If anything were to change, one would think that one's name would at least stay intact. One's name is the one constant in one's life, acquired at birth, and hangs around for quite some time after one has departed from this world. To me, my name summed up the essence of me … or so I thought.

For here in the US, I have learnt that it is a real struggle trying to hold on to my original name. In my first few months in the US, whenever I was asked for my name by an official or service personnel, I replied with great confidence.

"My name is Lee Su Kim."

Then came the strange, perplexing questions.

"What is your last name, Mam? Is it Kim?"

My initial reaction was to chuckle with laughter, thinking that the person was joking with me. Surely anyone who has had some contact with anything remotely Chinese or eaten Chinese food would know that Lee is a Chinese surname. Besides, aren't there, like, one billion Chinese in the world? But, as time went on, it began to dawn on me that there really was a problem here—many Americans do not understand the structure of a Chinese name!

To the Chinese, the surname is of paramount importance. It always comes first, followed by two more syllables which comprise the actual name of the person. The Chinese surname identifies one with an entire clan with the same surname and links you to your roots. In the United States, the common frame for a name is one's first name, a middle name (optional), then one's last name, for example, Billy Brown—Brown is the last name and Billy is the first name.

Not a problem, you might say. But for a Malaysian Chinese just arrived from Malaysia, where everyone of all races sort of know how our different names are aligned, it took some mental concentration to focus and remind myself that now my surname i.e. my first name was now my last name!

"What's your first name?" the American bank teller asked me when I tried to open a savings account.

"My first name? Err … it's Lee! Oh wait a minute … My first name is still Lee but now, over here, my first name is er … Su Kim and my original first name is now my last name Lee. Grooannnn …"

She looked at me blankly and said, "Mam, could you make up your mind, please?"

For a long while after my arrival in the US, I struggled valiantly to preserve my name in its original form. I could give up *sambal belachan, teh tarik*, but hey, I was NOT going to buckle under and change my name just because of this all-encompassing paradigm.

Well, after six months, I cracked under the weight of the system. I shifted my precious surname to the back instead of its former prestigious frontal position. This was because it was just too much hassle having to explain every time a misunderstanding occurred. Getting called Lee Su is no fun when one isn't named Lee Su.

"Hello, Lee Su. Could I interest you in making a small donation to the Paralyzed Veterans' Society?"

I would receive a telephone call from out of the blue. I don't

know how they get my name and phone number, but please, I am not a Lee Su.

"Excuse me, I am not Lee Su. My name is Su Kim and my surname is Lee."

Then a few minutes later, another call, "Hello, can I speak to Miss Kim?"

After months of having my name mauled to bits, of *sulees* and *leesus* and *kimlees*, and months of trying to educate name-manglers the structure and order of a Chinese name, I gave up.

If you can't beat them, join them, and so alas, I have to confess I am now Su Kim Lee over here. True to myself still but alas, somewhat mutated. Not yet hyphenated, and still resisting punctuation. (Many Chinese here hyphenate their names so that there is no confusion over their first and middle names, for example, Siew-Fen Teh.)

At a class last semester in the graduate studies programme I was attending, we all had to introduce ourselves briefly.

An Indonesian classmate introduced himself, "I have only one name. My name is Soekarno. No first name and no last name. But you can call me Ass!"

I saw some eyebrows shoot up but no one said anything. Everyone remained politely politically correct. After class, I could not contain my curiosity. I walked over and asked Soekarno softly why he said we could call him Ass. He replied in not-so-good English that he was fed up of having to explain that he had only one name, something not uncommon in Indonesia. Out of frustration, he decided to give himself a first name by taking the first letter of his name, 'S' for Soekarno.

"Oh," I muttered, and walked away.

He was about to leave for his homeland soon. Let the man return home in blissful innocence. Who was I to tell him that he had made an 'S' of himself in his choice of a name!

I am a Coloured Oriental Alien

My sojourn in the US revealed the power of words and how they can be wielded to serve peoples' purposes.

Just from the mere act of boarding a plane, travelling 20,000 miles to the US, and residing here, I find that my 'condition' has changed, even though outwardly I haven't at all physically. I now fit into certain categories, with certain labels, which would not have applied when I was home in Malaysia, although of course, over there, we have our own homemade labels too. You see, man has this need to categorise and compartmentalise—and how else but to slot us under 'labels'?

Here in the US, in a predominantly Anglo-White domain, I find myself slotted into some really bizarre categories. One weird one is this category called 'Peoples of Colour'. This would include all the peoples in the US who are 'more coloured' and visibly different (in terms of physical features and complexion) than the average Anglo-White American. Examples of such 'coloured peoples' are the Blacks, the Native Americans (or American Indians), brown-skinned Hispanics, the Asians, and the Pacific Islanders.

I was struck by how relative concepts can be because on

arrival here in the US, to my astonishment, I suddenly qualify for the slot of 'Peoples of Colour'. From 'Colourless' to 'Of Colour' in just a timespan of twenty-four hours! How strange to be suddenly called 'coloured' when in my homeland, the Chinese were considered the palest of the lot in the colourful melting pot of multicultural Malaysia.

On a personal level, I wouldn't disagree with this strange new expression—"a person of colour." This is because on an individual basis, I am definitely a 'Person of Colour'. I turn colour with the seasons in the US—from light brown in autumn, to a sun-starved beige-ish brown in winter, to caramel in spring, and butterscotch in summer when my highly active melanin pigmentation rises to the occasion.

I had always been the brownest Chinese girl in my school. Brown, I suppose, is a subjective concept too. Others might prefer to call me the most 'sunburnt' Chinese girl during my school days. Being of Baba Nyonya stock and being active in competitive swimming also contributed to a dusky complexion. Long vacations basking on the beaches of Port Dickson, a seaside resort, contributed further to a deeper tan.

My clan and I have no fear of the sun, and do not mind being browned by the sun. Most Straits Chinese have dusky-brown complexions like the Malays. However, while the Straits Chinese don't mind their kind being brown, the Chinese favour a fair complexion as the epitome of feminine beauty. I remember how I loathed being in certain company who viewed being brown somewhat like being over-toasted.

I used to cringe whenever I accompanied my mother to her local ladies hair-styling salon at Batu Road, run by a Madame Ling Ling, a Cantonese lady with a bouffant hairdo and pale white skin. Madame Ling and her equally pasty-white shampoo girls would stare at me and groan with dismay every time I stepped into the hair salon, especially after the long school holidays by the sea.

"Aiyohhhh … cho-meh kam hak-ah? Tai pai mou yen oi-loh." (Translation from Cantonese into English: "Aiyohhhh … why you so dark? Next time nobody want you …!")

They would cluck disapprovingly as they looked mortified at my sunbaked 'roastedness'. Their concern wasn't about the health and sun exposure factor but the correlation between one's colouring and the marriageability factor. To them, I was destined to be a condemned sunburnt old maid! They would touch me almost gingerly as they scratched my scalp and shampooed my hair as if my brownness would transfer itself to them. They would nag and lecture, "Who want you-oh next time? Very hard to find husband–oh! Why you no carry umbrella-ah?"

"Mou sai tow kam noong-ah," would be their parting words to me as we leave the salon, Mother sporting a brand new coiffure looking like Hong Kong movie star Lily Ho and I, glaring and bristling at them. (Translation of *"Mou sai tow kam noong-ah"*—"Don't sunbathe till so …" the only equivalent I can think of for *noong* is 'burnt toast'!) If only I had known then that Americans actually pay big bucks to get the tan which I sported for free, I would have told those permanently pale shampoo ladies a thing or two!

The other rather interesting label that I've come across here in the US is the term 'Oriental'. One day, in a multicultural education class, I was posed a question by my American professor that completely floored me. I had been in the US for only a semester and was attending a summer course.

We were seated in a circle when the learned Professor of Multicultural Education asked me, "So, Su Kim Lee, how do you feel about being an Oriental here in the US?"

"Huh? Oriental? Who me?" I muttered in surprise.

I looked around wondering whether he had meant the Korean students seated nearby. Surely he meant the Korean or the Japanese or even the Thai students. Me—an Oriental? He's got to be joking, I thought.

"Err … you mean I am considered an 'Oriental' here? This is the first time I've ever been called this term," I explained to my professor.

All my life, the word 'Oriental' bore connotations of … well, the Orient … the Far East, of almond-eyed maidens in *cheongsams*, pagodas, temples, paper umbrellas and Chinese junks. In fact, the word 'Oriental' has an exotic flavour to it and conjured visions of Suzy Wong, and *Flower Drum Song* which themselves are Hollywood-inspired. In Malaysia, when I used the word 'Oriental', I would use it to describe, say, a restaurant or an oriental ambiance. I never thought I'd be 'Oriental'! It was hard to explain that the region where I came from, i.e. Southeast Asia was quite different from the Far East to some of these geography-challenged Texans. To many 'Occidentals' in the US, if you have 'Oriental' features, then you are an 'Oriental'. It is not a pejorative term.

'Alien' was another word I had to get used too. When you have just arrived in the US, it takes some time before you get some kind of validation of your existence as you need to get the important stuff done such as telephone number, driver's licence number, social security number, bank account number, etc., anything that gets you numbers and proves that you 'exist'. If you do not hold a green card and you are residing in the US, you are called a Resident Alien. To me, the word, 'Alien' connotes images of green, big-headed, skinny-legged monsters from Mars, also Hollywood-sponsored I suppose, and it did take some getting used to the fact that I was now an Alien.

So lump them together and I become an 'Alien Oriental Person of Colour'. Vividly exotic and out of this world, I must say. Just a normal Malaysian Chinese woman, who gets into a plane and on arrival at destination, becomes alien, coloured, and Oriental. Wow! Who needs Hollywood? Clearly, middle mainstream America does.

My Anglo-American friend, Jim, says he doesn't understand why he's called White.

"I'm not white, I'm actually pink. I don't understand how I ended up being called White. Just look at me, am I white? How gross if I were really white in colour!" But we did agree that it would sound even funnier if the phrase were changed to 'Anglo-Pink.'

Another friend who's fourth generation American, born and bred in the US, says she takes issue with the phrase Native American as she considers herself as 'native American' as you can get. I wanted to tell her, hey, quit complaining … what about me? Back home in Malaysia, I am called a Non—a non-*bumiputera*, and I wasn't quite in the mood to explain how long my ancestors have been around on the soil of Malaysia, as I am sixth generation Straits Chinese.

Ah well … words … they're so convenient. How could we live without them? They help us to sort out and slot things and people into boxes, classify for tidiness and convenience, divide for execution and implementation. And in the process, some of us actually end up believing in 'them' labels too!

Hurray for Hollywood

I did not have a clue what Texas was like before I arrived. The only state I had ever visited in the US was Hawaii, a group of islands in the Pacific to the west of mainland North America. To me, Texas conjured images of cowboys rounding up cattle, rugged men in cowboy hats and faded blue jeans, lassos in hand, charging around on harummphing horses to the strains of the theme song from *Laredo*.

Cowboys were always laconic, long-legged dudes with taut buns that looked real good in their dusty denims, chatting up chanteuses dressed in flimsy blouses spilling over lovely brown shoulders. Cowboys didn't walk but strutted into honky-tonk bars, swing doors flapping, hands hovering above the guns poised at their hips, fingers itching for a deadly shoot-out. Somewhere at the bar, there was always the prerequisite native American (or 'Red Injun' as some people still call them), with sleepy doe-like eyes, dressed in a blanket with a feather or two on his head.

When I reached Texas, I thought, I would get to sip a Margarita at the long bars of Wild Wild West saloons, listen to good Country and Western music, while the wind howled outside, horses fidgeted nervously gnawing at their bridles, and clumps of tumbleweed tossed around on dusty streets. The saloon doors would swing apart, and suddenly, a Clint Eastwood-type with cigarette butt between his lips, would strut in … yes, that would quite make my day, I mused …

It was a very long journey from Kuala Lumpur as Houston was on the opposite side of the world from where I was originally located—a journey of twenty-four hours by plane, with a stop at Tokyo's Narita Airport, and another at Los Angeles before boarding a domestic flight to Houston. When I finally arrived in Houston, I was shocked to find a huge sprawling rather unattractive city, somewhat like the ugly cousin of the more sleek Dallas. The architecture was bland and boring, buildings were square, boxlike and unimaginative and there was an absence of greenery. It had a frontier feel, but where were the saloons, the enchanting senoritas and the James Deans? Where were the wild-eyed horses with flying manes and the stampeding wild buffaloes? Indeed, where were the cows? In my four years in Texas, except for the Rodeo that came to Houston annually, where you pay big money to watch cowboys ride bucking horses and brand cattle, I never saw nor bumped into a cowboy.

Only when I arrived in America did I realise that many of the constructs, ideas and impressions which I had of the US were in fact generated by Hollywood. It was really Hollywood and not America that has created so many myths in my head about a bold brash beautiful country, where one could speak freely without fear or favour, where the oppressed and the underprivileged had a fighting chance to achieve the American dream, where you can get rich and famous beyond your dreams. I thought I would see lots of beautiful people—gorgeous sexy women and good-looking hunks. I didn't encounter any.

Instead, I saw a lot of really fat people.

I realise now how much of a mythmaker Hollywood is, and how deluded the rest of the world is with Hollywood-created ideas and dreams of the US.

I am in the dark cinema watching the movie Entrapment, *starring Catherine Zeta Jones and Sean Connery. The story is set in Kuala Lumpur. They are going to stage a heist at the Petronas Twin Tower, located in the heart of Kuala Lumpur. I almost choke on my mountainous bag of popcorn when they show the actors cruising down a most foul looking, filthy river in a rickety old sampan.*

"Welcome to Kuala Lumpur," the actor says in the movie.

What? That is not Kuala Lumpur. I would know, because I was born and raised in Kuala Lumpur. I could recognise the scenery—that scene was filmed many miles away from KL in the city of Malacca and that dirty river was most certainly the Malacca River!

The plot in the movie thickens—the password required to enter the Petronas Twin Towers, the world's tallest building (at that time) is a Mandarin word. I chortle with laughter. Don't this people do their homework, I thought? A Malay or maybe an English password but a Mandarin word in the building built by Malaysia's National Oil Company? I don't think so … But then I remind myself—this is Hollywood, what do you expect?

I have no quarrels with Hollywood. It is the nature of the film industry to spin stories, enlarge fantasies, create dreams. It is the job of movies whether produced in Hollywood, Bollywood, London, Hong Kong, or anywhere in the world to entertain. Movies are a wonderful form of escapism. We just need to know, as movie goers, when to separate reality from film, fact from fiction. It is when we do not know that the worry begins.

I was introduced to the world of the old Hollywood movie classics when I was fourteen because of a nasty bump in the otherwise peaceful history of events in my country Malaysia. On 13 May 1969, parts of Kuala Lumpur went up in flames. Racial riots had broken out after the hotly contested political elections between the Malays and Chinese in certain parts of the city, incited by certain radical groups. I was just a teenager then, unaware of what hate was, nor even the concept of ethnicity. In fact, I had just watched a movie entitled *Great Expectations* at the School Hall along Bukit Bintang Road. The screening of the movie was organised by the School Prefects to raise money to help the underprivileged and it cost us a dollar to go and see the movie.

It was 4:30 P.M. The movie had just ended. I was sitting on the steps of the long spacious corridor of the Bukit Bintang Girls' School, waiting for my father to come and pick me up from school. It had been a wonderful film—based on Charles Dickens' famous story of the grotesque aging bride still in her bridal gown waiting for a wedding that never took place, and of Pip the brave little boy who has the strange encounter with the fading bride.

My father appeared grim-faced and told me that we had to go home immediately. I remember that scary journey. I could see thick acrid smoke in the distance, hanging over a once peaceful city that lost its innocence and descended into darkness that tragic day. Throughout the short journey home, I heard the wailing shrieks of police car sirens and ambulances as they raced crazily up and down the streets like dazed beetles. A curfew was imposed for several weeks in many parts of the country and a state of emergency was declared.

This meant there was no school for weeks. No homework,

no exams, nothing but a long stretch of time for relaxation and play. To a teenager, this certainly was an unexpected 'great expectation'. I remember watching the old Hollywood classics aired late at night on television. My mother loved the classics and I was thoroughly influenced by her infectious enthusiasm and ended up accompanying her night after night. She had grown up on these movies and it was a treat to be able to view them all over again. For me it was the first time. They were just marvellous.

We quaked and shivered as the beautiful Greer Garson tried to cling to her sanity in *Gaslight*, trembled as she was led to the gallows as Marie Antoinette, smiled at Claudette Colbert's predicaments in *It Happened One Night*, sighed over Audrey Hepburn's blooming romance in *Breakfast at Tiffany's*, sobbed with anguish when Ingrid Bergman had to leave Humphrey Bogart in *Casablanca*.

Sometimes Papa would join us too—Father, Mother and I would gape at Ava Gardner's smouldering beauty in *Mogambo*, marvel at how American movie stars like Jennifer Jones could look so good in *cheongsams* in *Love is a Many Splendoured Thing*, and gape at Elizabeth Taylor's stunning, oozing sex appeal in *Ivanhoe*. Papa always commented that Sophia Loren's lips were too thick and her mouth too wide and Liz Taylor was too dark and hairy for him. He liked the more classic beauties such as Rita Hayworth and Jean Simmons, but his favourite was the beautiful Chinese movie actress, Lin Dai.

My mother was a great movie aficionado. She could sing too. I learnt songs from the old movies such as 'Oh Rosemarie I Love You', 'I'll Be Calling You', and 'The Donkey Serenade' from Mama. She loved reciting Scarlett O'Hara's speech about never having to starve "as God is my witness" as long as one owned land and Tara—from our favourite movie, *Gone With the Wind*. Of course, both Mother and I could not resist mouthing aloud with Rhett Butler at the climax of the movie, "Frankly my dear, I don't give a damn," as the tempestuous Scarlett turns pale with fright at the thought of finding and simultaneously losing her true love.

"*Padan ee-eh bin,*" Ma would retort in a mixture of Malay and Hokkien, literally "Serves her face right" and then advise me in English, "See? Kim? Never take a man for granted. See what happens to her, *aiyohh ... kesian.*" (Poor thing.)

Mother had lots of favourite movie stars such as Clark Gable, Errol Flynn, Spencer Tracy, Jimmy Stewart, but her absolute favourite was Rock Hudson. He was tall, suave and handsome, with a great physique and a gentlemanly demeanour about him. Mama adored him and never missed a movie of his. One day, many years later, my sister, brother and I had some hilarious moments when my mother who was reading the newspapers suddenly threw the papers down in horror, pulled her bifocals off her nose in disgust, and started swearing.

"*Chee ... Chee ... Cheh! Celaka!*"

It seemed her movie idol, Rock Hudson had finally decided to come out in the open and had confessed that he was actually gay. My mum was no homophobe but to find out that one's secret hero was actually a closet gay, after all those years of girlish adoration lavished on him, was certainly quite a blow to her.

In the last month of our stay in the US, we decide to take a vacation to Los Angeles and San Francisco. We do the usual tourist sights in LA, and of course we visit Hollywood. We visit Grauman's Chinese Theatre, and walk down the famous Walk of Fame, one of Hollywood's most famous tourist attractions, where movie stars are immortalised by leaving their hand prints and footprints in the pavement for posterity, I was frankly a little disappointed—the place was unkempt and litter fluttered about Hollywood Boulevard. In fact, Hollywood seemed a tad tacky. I felt like my mother on finding out about Rock—a sense of disappointment—where was the glamour, the glitter, the beautiful people? The magic and romance of Hollywood were captured on celluloid, the mystique lay in our minds. The reality was very different.

Anna and the King *is playing at the elegant Egyptian Theatre in LA. We decide to catch the movie that evening. Jimmy, Jan Ming and I are seated comfortably in the theatre with its plush red velvet seats. Three young adults slip into the seats in front of us. I can tell they are Thai because they are speaking in Thai. They look like university students. The movie starts.*

As the movie runs on, the Thais in front of us seem to get more and more irate. Sometimes they chuckle with amusement, but most of the time, they are whispering and jabbering away in disbelief. I guess seeing a Hong Kong movie star, Chow Yun Fat, acting as the King of Siam is hard to take for them. The actors in the movie are actually speaking in Thai, including Mr. Chow Yun Fat. That must have really captured their attention. I sit up with a jolt—I recognise a number of well-known celebrities from Malaysia in the movie—there is Harith Iskandar as the guard, Mano Maniam as the aide to Anna, Shanthini Venugopal as his wife, and Deanna Yusof as the head wife of King Mongkut. How strange yet wonderful to see familiar Malaysian faces in a cinema in the heart of LA. I also recognise a number of scenes filmed in Ipoh, a town in North Malaysia.

Oh oh, the three Thais seem very agitated ... they walk out. Maybe they just want a cheeseburger, or maybe something in the movie has offended them deeply.

I feel like reassuring them—don't take it too much to heart. This is just Hollywood the myth maker. But then I remember how insulted the Thai people were by an earlier movie called The King and I, *where they featured Yul Brynner, as the King of Siam prancing around barefooted, waltzing to Rodgers and Hammerstein's 'Shall We Dance?' with the English governess in his arms. How would I feel if it were the King of Malaysia prancing around instead? Wouldn't I get offended too?*

This is Hollywood. Hollywood does not have overtly wicked intentions—it just wants to entertain. Perhaps a little facile and naive at times. Texas isn't a Land of Cowboys, I have learnt. All the impressions and illusions of Texas which I gleaned from the movies are largely churned from a mammoth film industry whose survival depends on the myths it creates. Nothing is quite like what Hollywood portrays it to be. Well, yes, as they say, Hurray for Hollywood.

Oh Well, Whatever

In my first semester at the university where I was undergoing a doctoral programme, I met a lovely American lady named Julia, who was taking the same course as me. We got along really well and soon became good friends. She was great fun, bright, witty and friendly. Every evening after class, we would walk together towards our cars a short distance away from the lecture hall, discussing the lecture, our work and enjoying each other's company.

One evening, as we bade farewell, she said, "Well, Bye, Kim Su. See you next week."

I was a little startled but then smiled at her mistake and said, "Hey, my name is not Kim Su. It's Su Kim."

She tossed her head nonchalantly, waved goodbye to me again, and said, "Kim Su, Su Kim. Oh well, whatever … they're all the same anyway," got into her car and drove away.

I stood there alone in the vast car park in the fading daylight, gulped down the lump in my throat, got into my car dejectedly, and drove the long haul home.

As I sped along the busy highway, through some rather unsavoury parts of Calhoun, then past the cluster of imposing skyscrapers in downtown Houston, I thought about Julia's blasè comment about my name, and Chinese names in general. Whereas "English" names or "Christian" names are so well-known and everyone is familiar with a Diana, a Janet or a Rosemary, the Chinese name, to the uninitiated, may sound like a meaningless cluster of three monosyllabic sounds. But the truth is they do have a meaning and an order.

The first name in a Chinese name is of course the all-important surname. This surname identifies you with one's roots and clan, and is the link between oneself and one's ancestors through the paternal line. A Chinese cannot choose his or her surname. You are born with it. It is only the middle and the last name that one can be creative with. The middle or last name can also identify you with your siblings and cousins. For example, my elder sister Su Win and I and all my female cousins from the paternal line have the middle name *Su*, which means Gift in Mandarin. My last name *Kim* means Gold and put together, my name means, 'A Gift of Gold' or 'Golden Gift'. My sister's name Su Win means 'Glorious Gift', my cousin Su See's name means 'Silken Gift', another cousin's name Su Mei means 'Beautiful Gift', and so on.

As my sister, the oldest in her generation, was named Su by my father, his brother and all his male cousins followed suit and named their daughters born into this Lee clan Su, followed by the last name of their own choice. Thus, my female cousins are Su See, Su Lan, Su Wan, Su Lee, Su Kwan, Su Mei, Su Lin, Su Ann, and more. The oldest boy of my generation in my clan was named Yu San and likewise, all the boys of that generation in the clan are named Yu something or other. If I returned to Malacca to visit my relatives there today and bump into someone called Yu Boon or Yu Chong or Yu Sui or Yu Yoong, he could very well be my cousin.

I found out one day that my name might not even have been Su Kim if not for something that happened in the family a long time ago.

When I was sixteen years old, I was chatting with my amah Chae Chae while she was ironing in the dining room. I enjoyed these chats with her, sniffing the warm pleasant toasty smell of newly pressed clothes, listening to the sizzle as the hot iron torched the freshly sprinkled garments. My amah blurted out a family secret that afternoon. It wasn't really a secret, just that no one ever talked about it and it had gotten lodged into an unspoken corner of our lives. My amah was telling me stories of poverty and suffering in her native China during the war-torn years, how on some days there was absolutely nothing to eat but rice mixed with a squirt of black soy sauce or mixed with boiled water. The Second World War and the Japanese Occupation of Malaya had also wreaked terrible destruction on the people of Malaya. She shared that the war had affected my family too, long before I was born.

"I only came to work with your family in 1953 when your elder sister was born. But I know that before her, there had been another baby born into this family just after the war years. Your mother told me so," Chae Chae nattered merrily away to me.

She revealed that I wasn't the second-born in the family, but actually the third child in the family.

I was stunned. How could this be? How was it that I didn't know about this? My amah looked at me and said that she didn't know the full story.

"I really don't know much. You will have to ask your Mother, *Mui Mui* (her pet name for me which means Little Sister)."

I went running around the house to look for Mama—out to the air well, the courtyard, through the middle hall and into the living room but she wasn't there. My family home, in a quiet street in the heart of Kuala Lumpur, was like one of those antique Straits Chinese houses you see along Jonker Street in Malacca or Peranakan Place in Singapore. It was an old, pre-war house, with beautiful Italian floor tiles, very high ceilings with exposed beams, an imposing red door at the entrance, and exquisite glass-stained windows in green, amber and blue. I bounded up the steep wooden staircase with the delicate green banisters, calling for her, and finally found Mama in her bedroom, putting away some clothes in her chest of drawers.

"Mama, is it true that I am not your second child?" I demanded to know with all the sensitivity of an adolescent.

She looked shocked, "Who told you this?"

"Chae Chae," I replied.

Her voice softened, "Yes, it's true," she sighed. A look of anguish swept over her features, and my heart almost stopped beating as she told me her story.

"I gave birth to your eldest sister—the sister whom you never knew—just after the war. The Japanese Occupation was over and everything was in disarray. We were told that the hospitals were ill-equipped, in shambles, that it was safer to give birth at home with a midwife in attendance. That decision was a bad mistake."

Mama hesitated, reluctant to revisit a painful event in her past. She heaved a deep sigh and continued, "A complication arose. My baby was born but she had suffocated to death. If I had given birth in the hospital, perhaps she could have been saved. But who can tell? Your sister, had she lived, would be in her mid-twenties by now."

I was astonished. I had a sister. A sister I never knew, never heard spoken of until now.

"But why didn't you or Papa ever tell us?" I asked in dismay.

"What's the use? What's the point of wallowing in the past? Why keep remembering something you want to forget? It was just too painful to remember," Mama muttered.

There was a wistful sadness in her eyes. I felt as if I had intruded on a deep and private sorrow. I began to understand just an inkling of the tragedy that must have taken place in this room a long time ago.

"She was so beautiful," Mama continued. "She was a full-term baby, perfectly formed and just so beautiful ... There was nothing wrong with her at all except that it had taken too long for her to come out and she had suffocated inside me. I took one look at her before they took her away. She looked as if she were just asleep. Her eyes were closed, she had the biggest eyes ... I could tell by the sweep of her eyelashes ... right across her face and upwards. Papa and I were heartbroken."

"She had a name too. Her middle name was Oi which means 'Love' in Chinese. We hadn't yet decided on the last name. There was no reason for her to die ... just no reason at all ..." she said softly.

I did not know what to say. I did not know much about babies at that time nor had I even encountered death. All I learnt was that I had another sister besides my sister, Su Win. And I felt terrible to have made Mama so sad in my impulsive need to know.

As I crept quietly out of the room, at a loss for the right words to say, Mama called out to me, "Kim, actually you're not my third child ... you're the fourth. After the death of your oldest sister, I conceived again a few years later but had a miscarriage. That was when we decided to give up the name Oi—too much bad luck."

"When I finally was in the family way again, we decided on the name Su which means Gift. When your sister was born, we called her Su Win. That change in name brought us good luck. After that, you and then your brother came along," she brightened up a little.

"So we have been blessed, no need, you see, to hang on to the past. You must understand that life's like that, not always good and happy things but in everyone's life, tragedy and sadness will visit too. You cannot know happiness until you have experienced sadness."

I stumbled out of the room, my emotions in turmoil. Like Mama, I too wanted to move on, close those pages, leave them untouched. That fateful day, I learnt that two siblings of mine never made it. And if they had, with three children in the family, perhaps there wasn't any need to have me. Perhaps, I wouldn't have existed.

So you see, my dear friend, Julia, our names are not all the same. They aren't just a bunch of clanging Chinese syllables. They have meanings and some even have stories behind them. No 'whatever' about it.

Shoot Down the Moon, Mama!

My son Jan Ming was only five years old when we arrived in Houston in 1996. The private school where we enrolled him for his primary school education required him to sit for a placement exam. It was going to be a simple oral exam, we were told. Parents were not allowed in this exam. As we handed over our little boy to one of the American teachers, I worried how he was going to understand her strong Texan drawl. She took him by his hand and led him away to one of the rooms. Trustingly he followed her, a little puzzled as to what all the fuss was about.

After thirty minutes, the teacher appeared with Jan Ming. He had passed the test and would certainly have a place in the school, she said. He had performed quite well in the test, but he seemed baffled over two questions. I asked her what they were.

She drawled in a strong nasal twang,

"Well, Mam, he couldn't describe how to make a sandwich! A simple sandwich. It looks as if he has never heard of a sandwich before."

"But he's a clever little boy," she hastily assured me, "He muttered something about putting things between slices of bread!"

She added, "The second question was 'How to Run a Bath'."

"Run a what?" I asked.

"Run a bath. You know, how to fill up a bathtub when you want to soak in the bath. I gave him some clues like turning on the faucet. He seemed even more confused."

"Turn on a what?" I asked.

I had never heard the word 'faucet' being used before.

"A faucet, Mam … you know, a faucet, the thing you turn on to get running water," she looked at me as if I were equally dumb, a chip off the same block.

I said, "Oh you mean a tap! You know something? Your questions are not very culturally sensitive. I think we are talking about different varieties of English here. We don't say faucet in Malaysia. We say tap. We use British English in my country, you know the Queen's English … I think only Americans use this word 'faucet'."

She seemed flabbergasted—'culturally sensitive'? What's wrong with these strange people—what's sandwiches and bathing got to do with culture? And 'tap', ain't that a dance?

That evening, I reflected on Jan Ming's first American exam and mused that he had never made a sandwich in his life. This was because we were privileged enough to have a maid from the day he was born and he never had to prepare any food for himself. Even if we did not have a maid, I reckon I would have been the 'maid' preparing the food. Secondly, he didn't like sandwiches very much, preferring soft-boiled eggs and *nasi lemak* for breakfast. In school, he purchased hot meals and snacks at the local school canteen. Jan Ming's American school canteen, I noted, had peanut butter and jelly sandwiches, peanut butter sandwiches, as well as ham, egg and cheese sandwiches

on its menu. That took some getting used to, as we are used to hot meals for lunch and having to eat a cold sandwich for lunch made me quite miserable initially.

As for bathing, there are actually other ways of bathing apart from the Western bathtub style of bathing. The most wonderful way in hot tropical countries is also a big tub of water but the difference is that you do not climb into the tub, but bathe outside it! Using a ladle, you pour ladles of cold water from the big tub on to yourself. This is absolutely refreshing on a hot, sticky, sweaty day and highly recommended rather than soaking in a blistering hot tub.

Most homes in urban areas in Malaysia have showers, many also have Western–style bath tubs (some indulge in Jacuzzis) in their bathrooms but my five-year-old was befuddled when asked to run a bath because he had never bathed inside a tub nor run a bath. He was used to the shower and the big *hum tun kong* (an antique pot with gold dragon motifs originally used to store salted eggs from China) of water in his bathroom, and the occasional crazy splashing about like a beached whale whenever he encountered a big bath tub in the bathrooms of luxury hotels.

Jan Ming and I took a walk in the neighbourhood that night. It was a full moon. The moon was in full splendour, a glowing orb in the dark blue sky. It hung so low you could reach out and unhinge it from the sky over Texas.

I sighed. The full moon brought back memories of my home and folks faraway.

I noticed Jan Ming dancing around on the pavement, looking up open-mouthed with wonder at the huge glowing moon.

My heart went out to him ... how would he cope in this new country? Would he be placed in the 'dud' class for not answering those two 'critical' questions?

"Oh look, look at the moon, Mama," Jan Ming yelled.

I didn't answer.

He looked at me as if sensing my mood, and said, his eyes twinkling with humour, "Let's shoot down the moon, Mama, to make Mooncakes."

I gave my little boy a big hug. I figured if he could be so creative with his words, why worry about sandwiches and bath tubs!

Help! 911!

On my very first weekend in Houston, I was having a meal with the family at a restaurant at the upmarket Galleria shopping mall. My son who was just five years old then, was giving me a real hard time, fretting and fussing over his food. The little monster refused to eat what he had ordered and began to throw a tantrum.

"I dowan, I dowan to eat! I wan Coca Cola."

I had tried gentle persuasion, soft cooing and coaxing and it hadn't worked so far. He was really stressing me out with his unnecessary whining. I gave him a smack on the back of his head.

My little boy glowered, his face puckering up as if not quite decided whether to use this opportune moment to yell and scream and indulge in a full blown tantrum or to just shut up and behave. However, it was my husband's behaviour that astounded me instead.

He started hissing, "Don't, don't, Kim, don't—"

"Don't what?" I asked incredulously.

Jan Ming decided to launch into a howl, and Jimmy fidgeted nervously in his seat.

"Don't hit him! You will get into trouble here. You are not

supposed to hit your children here in the US. Someone might just report you." Jimmy frantically advised me.

That's a startling revelation. Am I not in the US—the supposed Land of the Free? What's this? I can't even discipline my child without someone spying on me?

"What? You're kidding. Who sez so?" I shot back.

"I know so. My colleagues told me so."

"Then how do I discipline him?"

"Try talking."

I tried talking.

"Look here you little *hantu* (Malay for 'devil'), if you scream some more, I will give you one tight slap."

"Shhussh. Lower your voice please. Don't make threats that you can't keep …" the little *hantu's* father lectured me.

It was my second day in the US. When in a new country, there is always bound to be some adjustment, a bit of culture shock, I tell myself. But this was really worrying. A whack on the head or a smack on the hand doesn't exactly turn me into some abusive Asian mother or some she-wolf. It wasn't even painful in the first place, just a jolt to ensure that the pecking order was pointed out and that Junior knew his place and would grow up to be a well-behaved gentleman. We loved our little boy and very seldom ever laid a hand on him, but occasionally a smack helped to enforce some kind of discipline especially when all the words in the world would not work.

I learnt that this was the way in the US—you cannot whack your kids or else you might land in trouble with the authorities for child abuse. In my upbringing, my parents seldom ever laid hands on us. My siblings and I grew up in a household full of love and devoted parental affection. Only occasionally when we were rude or behaved really badly, we would get a smack or a knock on our head. Mother kept a *rotan* (a cane) in the storeroom and would threaten to use it sometimes if we were way out of line. Usually, just the threat of the much feared *rotan* was enough to get us to change our behaviour.

Once I remember after school, instead of walking straight home from school, about a twenty minutes' walk away, I decided to take a short detour to visit my best friend nearby at Hicks Road, near Ceylon Hill. In my excitement I forgot to inform my parents. Back then, there was no such thing as mobile phones nor SMS. I had a wonderful time at my friend's place and when I finally got home, I learnt that my parents were frantic with worry and had gone out in the car to scour the roads looking for me. When they finally came home without finding me, there I was in the sitting room, grinning at them. Out came the *rotan*, my Mum at one end of it, warning me never to do such a thing again —not informing them as to my whereabouts.

Even then I didn't really get whacked, as my amah would rush out to shield me from the *rotan*, putting her arms up like a mother hen, with me hiding and squealing behind her stout tubby physique, and Mama swishing the *rotan* at her legs. After a few more perfunctory swishes of the *rotan*, Mama would give up, pretending to scold my amah for being such an interfering busybody, make some more ominous warnings to me and then put the cane back in the store.

I guess things get easier with each passing generation. Discipline was even more strict during my parents' time. My maternal grandmother, according to my mother, was a tough disciplinarian, and bought up her brood of five girls and two boys based on the well known adage, 'Spare the rod and spoil the child'. Strict discipline was enforced at all times and the children got a beating on their legs with the *rotan* if they misbehaved.

The boys had to help out with the chores and the girls were trained in the culinary arts and household management skills. A Nyonya was supposed to master the culinary skills in order to become a good wife and mother one day. Food had to be prepared the Peranakan way, the *sambal* (chilli paste) had to be pounded just the right way with the right rhythms, the vegetables for the *nasi ulam* or *ju hu char* had to be cut into delicately thin strips, julienned as finely as possible. The flavours, taste and presentation were all important. If a cube of potato was too hideously chunky, or a strip of turnip or lettuce was too gawky, they would get a smack on their hands. Or Grandma would pull out her hairpin from her *sanggul* (hair swept into a bun) and give the erring *tak senonoh* (Malay for 'unladylike') young Nyonya a painful poke in the clumsy hand. No wonder all of them became such great cooks.

My favourite story from my mother was that of her two brothers during the Japanese Occupation of Malaya. Survival was really tough and they had to live on meagre rations of rice and *ubi kayu* (sweet potato). Because of the war, my mother's and her siblings' education was disrupted. There was no school to attend. To make ends meet, Grandma who was an excellent cook, made Nyonya cakes to sell. My Mum and her sisters helped their mother to make the cakes in the early hours of the morning. Then the two boys, Yat Kee and Yat Chin, had to go around on the family's only bicycle to sell the Nyonya *kueh* (cakes).

One morning, after a fresh batch of *kueh* was ready, the two brothers, in their early teens then, teetered out on the old bicycle, with Yat Kee pedalling furiously and Yat Chin, the younger brother, riding pillion and the precious tray of *kueh talam*, *kueh bengka* and *onde-onde* strapped on the back of the bicycle. However, they were in such a happy carefree mood, whizzing around on the bicycle, they did not realise the tray had not been properly secured and somewhere along the way, all the *kueh* had fallen off! When they finally found out, it was too late. They went home sheepishly, trembling in fear, without any money nor any *kueh*. They got a real hiding from Grandma. Till today, my two uncles reminisce fondly about the incident and chuckle over it.

Here, in the US, my son was enrolled in a private school in a quiet upmarket suburban area of Houston. The teachers there treated their charges with such love and affection. Jan Ming was called Sweetie, Darling, Sweetheart, Love and Honey by his teachers all the time from Year One to Four. Every task he performed was rewarded with stickers of stars and flowers, glowing comments, awards, ribbons, cuddles and more terms of endearment. This must have been a real pleasant culture shock to the child after attending school back in Malaysia where the favourite words of the class teacher to the schoolchildren were, *'Diam!'*, *'Jangan bising!'*, and *'Duduk dan tutup mulut!'* ('Keep quiet!', 'Don't make noise!' and 'Sit down and shut up!').

In his new American school, the underlying philosophy was to nurture the children's creativity and foster confidence through a culture of loving positive encouragement. Show-and-Tell sessions encouraged each child to come up to the front of the class to talk briefly on whatever they had brought to school, be it a leaf or a toy. Children were not talked down to, but treated as individuals with their own rights. The seating format was in clusters of desks and not the rigid format of desks in straight lines facing the blackboard. Verbalising, social interaction with peers, asking questions in class were always encouraged. Apart from academic work there were field trips, creative projects, cultural awareness projects, cultural celebrations, school concerts. Needless to say, he loved his new school and his teachers.

I realised Jimmy wasn't pulling my leg when he said one has to be careful in the US when disciplining one's child. Just a week after Jan Ming started school in the US, he came home from school, his eyes twinkling in delicious glee, announcing triumphantly he had a secret telephone number.

When I asked him what this number was, he smiled and said, "My teachers gave us a telephone number to call. If anything goes wrong at home, we must call 911!"

Throughout my four years' stay there, I had to walk the thin red line between the American way and the more traditional way of bringing up a child. Sure, words, coaxing and logic were used as often as possible, but sometimes, when the child is totally way out of line and you are worried sick that he will grow up to be a spoilt little brat, then there is nothing as effective as one good whack.

But I remember I had to close all the windows and doors first (lest the neighbours hear), then chase the little brat all around the house while he teased me and hollered, "911! Helllppppp … I'm going to call 911!"

This Thing Called Sue

"Wow, Mam, you sure are brave."

"You are so brave, Kim"

"My, you sure have guts."

I had been in Texas for only two months. It was my son's sixth birthday and I thought it would be a good idea to throw a birthday party for him at home. It would also be a good way of getting to know his friends and their parents. Invitation cards were sent out and one Sunday afternoon in the middle of December, Jan Ming's party was all set.

However, a strange thing happened. Every time the doorbell rang and a child was dropped off, a parent or so would mutter something about this quality called bravery. Then, they would head back for their cars and drive away with worried or bemused expressions on their faces. A nagging hunch I had was that they didn't seem to be worried about their child, rather they seemed worried for me!

What on earth was wrong with them? I was puzzled. What is so brave about throwing a party? I wasn't hosting a party for the Governor of Texas (who happened to be George W. Bush at that time). It was just a birthday party for six-year-olds.

After the last guest had been dropped off at my home, to my astonishment, the children suddenly went berserk. The boys started screaming and yelling and charged all around the house. Two of them tore into the master bedroom and started bouncing on the king-sized bed as if it were the neighbourhood trampoline. Some ran up and down the stairs charging in and out of every room. A few others grabbed the balloons which I had decorated around the house and proceeded to burst as many as they could. The loud popping of the balloons didn't seem to scare anyone except the birthday boy who started to cry. The girls were having a tussle on the sofa, and started a pillow fight with my cushions.

It was as if they had all gone wild simply because there wasn't any parental control. I had never seen such weird behaviour from children before at birthday parties back home. I was gradually beginning to understand why some of the parents muttered about guts and valour when they dropped off their kids.

"What's your Mum's name, Jan Ming?" one of the children asked my son.

"Mama ... er ... I mean, Su Kim."

"SU KIM! SU KIM! Can I have some Coke?"

Why, the precocious little thing calling me by my first name ...!

"Hey little boy, don't call me by my name. I'm much older than you. I'm as old as your Mum. You have to call me Aunty."

The ginger-haired, freckled boy looked at me up and down, stupefied, and scoffed out loud, "But you're NOT my Aunt! Why should I call you Aunty?"

"Hee hee," the others nearby all tittered, and laughed with glee.

Before I could explain that in my culture, it was not about

being blood relatives but simply courtesy to address seniors with honorifics like Aunty, the monsters were staging a little mutiny.

"We want Coke, we want Coke, we want Coke," they chanted.

"Okay, okay, you little *hantus* ...," I muttered under my breath.

Forget all the wonderful food I had prepared—the beautifully garnished fried *mee hoon* (rice noodles), the Nyonya Birthday Noodles, the dainty Top Hats laced with slivers of crab meat, the crispy wontons, the colourful *agar-agar* (jelly) inside handpainted egg shells, the prawn cutlets based on my grandpa's recipe—given to him from a Hainanese chef—the fruit punch, the fruit juices.

Okay, okay, stuff yourselves silly with sugary drinks, go on an almighty sugar buzz, don't blame me if you get too bloated to eat. No wonder there are so many obese people around in the US, I mumbled under my breath.

Next time ..., if there were a next time, ... if I survived this ..., a menu of just Coke, cheese pizza and fries would suffice, I made a mental note.

The party was supposed to be from 4 to 6 P.M., but it felt like the longest two hours of my life. At 6 P.M., the parents came to collect their children, and the ordeal ... er, I mean the party ended.

"Thank you, I had a great time," piped one chubby lad.

"Thank you ... err, Aunty ... Maybe next year?"

Yeah, right, I smiled (what I hoped was a smile), and waved the ginger-haired terror goodbye. With all the energy expended, some had morphed into little angels again. The children were all safely ferried home, and no mishaps had occurred. It dawned on me then that if anything had happened, if a child had choked on a pretzel or a fried wonton, tripped over the carpet, or fallen off the bannister, why, I could have been sued to kingdom come. I had quite forgotten, before the party, that the United States of America is the most litigious society in the world.

The number of lawyers in the US today is estimated to be around a million. With so many lawyers, filing millions upon millions of lawsuits monthly, suing has become the American way of life. 'Sue or be sued' is the relentless mantra of countless newspaper advertisements, tacky billboard ads, and the yellow pages. Hundreds of thousands of lawyers scheme and manipulate daily, seeking creative and ingenious means of suing the pants off someone. Anybody can sue anyone over anything any time they like. One can read about all kinds of litigation cases in the papers. The lawsuits get more and more entertaining, wacky or ingenious by the day. Here are some examples:

A woman filed a lawsuit against a television company and its weatherman for about $ 1,000 because of an erroneous forecast. The weatherman had predicted sun, but it rained instead. The rainstorm, said the woman, caused her flu and resulted in four days' missed work and $ 38 in medication.

A woman filed a lawsuit against the manufacturer of the golf cart from which her husband fell to his death after he had been drinking during a tournament at a local country club. She claimed the cart did not have seat belts and doors. Her son was driving the cart so she sued him too.

A man, 37 years old, filed a lawsuit against some state officials for a failed suicide attempt. He sued for injuries suffered when he fell and hit the concrete after his bedsheet had become unfastened as he jumped out a jailhouse window trying to hang himself.

A twenty-one-year-old man, who led police on a high-speed chase before crashing into a utility pole, sued the town as well as the police. He claimed that the five officers were responsible for his injuries because they violated a police department policy to discontinue high-speed pursuits when the risk exceeded the need for immediate apprehension.

A convenience store worker was awarded a whopping $ 2 million in punitive damages after she injured her back opening a pickle jar!

That explains why American manufacturers put all kinds of warnings, instructions and labels on their products, some of which border on the subliminally absurd. If you want some free laughs, just browse around in the huge supermarkets and malls and read the labels. My favourites are as follows:

On a blanket from Taiwan:
Not to be used as protection from a tornado

On a hair dryer:
Do not use in shower

On a brand of bread pudding:
Product will be hot after heating

On an American Airlines packet of nuts:
Instructions—open packet, eat nuts

On some frozen dinners:
Serving suggestion: Defrost

Can of self-defence pepper spray warns:
May irritate eyes

Baby stroller warning:
Remove child before folding

Warning on underarm deodorant:
Do not spray in eyes

Household iron warns:
Never iron clothes while they are being worn

Toilet bowl cleaning brush warns:
Do not use orally
Instructions for an electric thermometer:
Do not use orally after using rectally

In the manual of a chain saw:
Do not attempt to stop the blade with your hand

Duh-uh!

On Being Politically Correct

I had always envisioned the US of A as the Land of the Free, a place where freedom of speech prevailed. A place where one can say anything one likes without fear or favour, where you do not have laws like ISA and OSA or this Act or the other. No need to look over the shoulder or wonder if Big Brother is listening. No need to fear that someone will come a-knocking at your door in the middle of the night and whisk you away to incarceration without a trial. A country where you can spoof your president, lampoon your politicians, where there is absolute tolerance of whatever your beliefs and convictions are and the freedom to express them.

Well, being in America, I must say that I do admire the informality, the lack of stuffiness and protocol and an absence of feudalistic structures that seem to plague some of the societies in my part of the world. But total freedom of speech? Not when there is something called PC or political correctness. Gee, these Americans sure are touchy and prickly about some things. I found out to my consternation that it wasn't very nice nor polite to use the word 'old'. Apparently there is no such thing as old. Old people do not grow old, they just sort of well, progress in age. If one uses the word 'old' or call people old, then one is guilty of ageism.

I learnt this firsthand when I was invited to give a talk by the Malaysia America Society on my books *Malaysian Flavours* and *Manglish* at Washington, DC. The talk was very well-received and I think the audience loved it. Some of them were laughing till they had tears in their eyes as I talked about some features of Malaysian culture, the idiosyncrasies of Malaysians, Malaysian English, and other unique Malaysianisms to an audience comprising Malaysians and people who had lived in Malaysia before. Then I moved on from humour to personal reflections. I commented that as we grow older, we see things from a different perspective. Ageing has many advantages if one chooses to recognise them, one of which is one learns to let go of a lot of things and issues that used to be so important when one was young.

A man who looked like he was in his mid-seventies put up his hand and said, "Can you not use the word 'old', please?"

I was startled. I did not realise that I had offended some sensibilities in the audience. The Malaysians did not seem to mind at all when I talked about age and the wisdom of age, and were smiling and nodding in agreement with me, but I wasn't so sure of the others, particularly some of the Americans in the audience.

I apologised but then made sure I went on to share that it was a cultural thing. In my culture and in Malaysian society, 'oldness' wasn't anything to be embarrassed about, or to ignore. On the contrary, age and seniority were highlighted. I was brought up to respect old people. Seniority was equated to wisdom. Old people were always the first to sit down at the dinner table before others could take their seats, and given the most respect. I remember as a child, in a Peranakan household, my siblings and I were trained to 'address' each relative seated at the table before we could eat our food. We had to 'call' our grandparents followed by my parents before we could tuck into the yummy food. I would have to say, *"Koong Koong makan, Popo Makan, Papa makan, Mama makan"* in Baba Malay. This meant "Grandfather eat, Grandmother eat, Father eat, Mother eat" in English. It was not a command to one's folks to eat, but rather a ritual indicating that one was about to start one's meal and asking for the adults' blessings and permission to do so. If there were guests, we were trained not to start eating until we had addressed all the adults at the table, in order of seniority.

If we neglected to observe this ritual, along would come a sharp reprimand from my mother in front of everyone, *"Bay heow keow-ah?"* (Hokkien for "Don't you know how to 'call'?").

This was terribly embarrassing so we would rather get through the ritual quickly than lose face and be regarded as *kurang ajar* (Malay for 'not brought up properly') which indicated loss of face for the entire family, far too much to bear over something as simple as sitting down for a meal.

Thus, one was singled out for the number of years one lived and accorded the due respect and one's 'oldness' was never hidden but publicised. For someone culturally conditioned to defer to age and seniority, it was strange for me to be in a society where one does not openly acknowledge a person's old age when he or she was so obviously older than the rest. It wasn't that the Americans do not respect age. Not at all—just that it is seen as being politically incorrect if one points out another's old age, instead of highlighting it as in my culture.

I looked at the senior gentleman who had objected to being called 'old'. He had such a noble, dignified demeanour.

I wished I could convey to him at that moment my sense of awe and respect for him, his elegant mannerisms instead of the gauche clumsiness and haste of youth, his distinguished looks, his silver-white hair, even the wrinkles and furrows he wore on his face. How many stories and experiences he must have to share, he looked like someone who had aged graciously through the vagaries and challenges that life throws at each of us. How much wisdom he must have acquired in his life's journey, I reflected. Why oh why, Sir, I thought, would you ever want to object to the beauty and power of your 'oldness'?

"What word would you use for 'old' then, Sir?" I asked the old gentleman politely.

He was caught off-guard by my question, as if he had never been asked something like that before.

"Well, you could use … er … er …" he answered, lost, forced to confront reality or the simple truth.

Then he smiled, a twinkle in his eye. He winked at me and said, "I suppose you could use … er … 'advanced' instead of old."

"Okay, I will. Thanks," I said respectfully, returning his charming smile. I was nonplussed—'advanced' sounded even older than 'old', but I respected his feelings and avoided mentioning the word 'old' again.

I realised that this was the political correctness (PC) movement and using inappropriate terms or words pertaining to gender, ethnicity and age could be misconstrued as sexism, racism and ageism. The political correctness movement erupted in the 1980s in the wake of the communist collapse in Europe. It was based on a widespread declaration that certain ideas, behaviour and expressions should be forbidden by law and those who transgressed it should be punished. The declared rational of the PC movement was to prevent people from being offended, to avoid using words that may upset women, homosexuals, non-whites, the handicapped, the mentally impaired, the fat, the short or the ugly. Someone who is blind is called 'visually impaired' in PC, a deaf person is 'hearing impaired', a stupid person is not stupid but 'mentally challenged'. In short, a whole load of euphemisms are used instead of plain speak.

Sometimes this political correctness movement rears its ugly or pretty head, depending on how you feel about it, when you least expect it. For example, a university in Texas chose the theme Frontier Fiesta as the theme of its convocation celebrations. The university planned to set up stalls with a Wild Wild West theme, with the dress theme of Cowboys and Indians and planned to have food, games and events all carrying a Wild West flavour. However, this decision met with strong opposition from a small group of students who complained in the university newsletter that the theme of Frontier Fiesta carried connotations and reminders of oppression, cruelty and conquest of ethnic minorities, in particular the Native American tribes who were largely wiped out by the Anglo-Americans as they expanded their frontiers westwards. In the face of these objections, the theme was eventually diluted to something to do with Fiesta Celebrations minus the Frontier word.

Another instance was when the US government wanted to erect a statue of Franklin Roosevelt for the new Franklin Roosevelt Memorial in Washington DC. There were objections to the finished product. Although it was an outstanding beautifully-crafted bronze statue of the former President of the United States, there was criticism from the disabled and handicapped communities in the US. Roosevelt was handicapped—he was lame and moved about in a wheelchair but the statue did not feature this handicap. This was deemed to be an insult to the Disabled community as if one's handicap was something to be ashamed of, and they demanded that the statue portray him as in his real life, in a wheelchair. Even a simple innocuous Taco Bell commercial of a little Chihuahua running around with a bandage round its skinny little neck had the spasmodic neck-impaired people up in arms protesting against the advert.

I realised then that here in the US, there wasn't total freedom of speech. Why, I could be sued if I wasn't more careful in my speech. I come from a country which hadn't quite hooked onto the PC movement. Our vernacular languages and our own variety of English, namely Manglish, were rife with all kinds of politically incorrect words such as Pondan, Ah Kwa, Ah Beng, Ah Lian, Ceena Ah Pek, Sotong, Jinjang Joe, Mak Nenek, Anak Dara Tua, Buaya, Lembu, Ali Baba and so on … A lot of these names have connotations of sex, race, gender, ethnicity, disposition, handicaps, but we enjoy sprinkling them around in our conversations, and it would be a sad day if PC wiped these colourful expressions from our repertoire of languages. While we cannot talk openly about quite a lot of things in case we incite racial misunderstanding, and our arts and media cannot touch on issues such as sex, race, politics and religion which pretty much leaves nothing much left to talk about, we are horribly PC-unsavvy. Thus the average Malaysian will not hesitate to ask you, "Why you still not married-ah?" or "How much are you earning?" Or "How come so long you still don't have children-ah?" More sophisticated urban types would of course have picked up some PC-ness but most of the time, rightly or wrongly, we indulge in calling a spade a spade, without realising we are offending anyone's sensitivities.

More Close Encounters of the PC Kind

My second experience with political correctness in the US was even more bewildering. In the summer of my first year in the US, I enrolled for a course in Programme Evaluation in the doctoral programme at the university. On the first day, I stepped cheerfully, with a sense of happy expectancy, into the classroom. I noticed that all my classmates were Anglo-Whites. There were no international students at all in the course. That didn't trouble me at all as I enjoyed making friends and had lots of American friends. The strangest thing about this class was that although it was quite apparent to all that I definitely wasn't a homegrown American nor an ABC (American-born Chinese)—because I did not have an American accent—but someone from another part of the world, no one, absolutely nobody, acknowledged that fact.

To my mounting distress, no one came up to me to say hello or express any kind of personal interest as to who I was or where I came from. Everyone tried to be so politically correct by not acknowledging my difference. Acceptance of cultural or ethnic diversity lay in not enquiring about my origins but instead, in silent acceptance of my presence there. I, on the other hand, perceived it differently. I felt that by not expressing an interest in me and where I was from, there was non-acceptance of me. This took place from the beginning to the end of the course.

In my homeland, if you were a foreigner, Malaysians, being a curious lot, would without any hesitation, come up to you and ask you a barrage of questions such as, "Where are you from?" "What's your name?" "Where are you staying?" After that would come the perfunctory questions like "When did you arrive?" and "How long have you been here?" and eventually the mandatory "Have you tried durians?" and "Can you take spicy food?" This interest is without intention of being nosey or rude but sincerely expresses one's interest in the new kid on the block or the stranger in town. Showing interest in the foreigner conveys a sense of acceptance and a warm welcome to the foreigner.

Here in my strange summer class, I went through the whole semester without anyone ever asking me anything about me. Was it because I was in a university in Texas? Would it have been different if I had been in a more cosmopolitan, less insular part of the US, I have often wondered. Perhaps being used to safe, pasteurised American Anglo-White homogeneity, my Texan classmates didn't know how to handle a walking breathing whiff of cultural heterogeneity.

Political correctness was couched in not wanting to offend. My classmates did not want to offend, so they took pains not to convey any recognition of my ethnic difference. I appreciated that. But by their silent, unquestioning inclusion of me, I ended up in a perennial state of exclusion, miserable that no one was interested in my uniqueness as someone from a different culture with so much to share.

While this second encounter was a bland and colourless experience, my response to my third PC encounter was one of annoyance. This time it was the Asians living in

Houston who were being PC. My son's school celebrated the various American celebrations and festivals such as Valentine's Day, Christmas, Memorial Day, Independence Day, Easter, Hanukkah and Halloween. Our favourite celebration was Halloween which was quintessentially American. Every Halloween, the school would hold a celebration and decorate its classrooms with all kinds of bizarre Halloween decorations such as cobwebs, spiders, witches, brooms, jack-o'-lanterns, ghoulish masks, devils and devices emitting weird sounds such as the shrieking of banshees, howling and eerie cackles of laughter. Residents would dress up the front of their homes and yards with Halloween paraphernalia.

Halloween is fascinating to a newcomer to the US—when night descends on the eve of Halloween, children in all kinds of bizarre spooky costumes come out and go from door to door Trick-or-Treating. My son loved going Trick-or-Treating with his two American friends, Lenny and Chris. Dressed as goblins, ghosts, the Grim Reaper or Black Ninjas, they would go around the neighbourhood, pressing doorbells and chanting:

Trick or Treat
Smell my feet
Give me something good to eat

Obliging parents handed out sweets and chocolates and the boys were ecstatic over the huge pile of goodies at the end of the night, much to the chagrin of parents and the delight of dentists.

I noticed something odd in my fourth and final year of my stay in the US when I visited Jan Ming's school on Halloween day. The school had cut down its decorations to just banners with words like 'Happy Halloween' and jack-o'-lanterns. The broomsticks and scary stuff were eerily missing! When I inquired why the decorations were so muted that year, I was told that the school wanted to be culturally sensitive and did not want to offend any community's beliefs. It seemed some Chinese parents had objected to the Halloween decorations because the presence of brooms, ghosts, demons, devils and black colour was bad luck to the Chinese whose children were studying in that school.

I found this really disturbing. How can one community water down another's celebrations? Either you participate or you don't. And if you don't, surely one ought to respect the celebrations of others non-judgmentally. If everyone watered down or toned down their celebrations, imagine how colourless and homogenised all our festivals and celebrations would become!

As a Chinese myself, I was well aware of how superstitious the Chinese are about brooms. During Chinese New Year, it is considered bad luck to sweep one's house as it would mean sweeping away one's luck. The Chinese also consider it as 'soiay' (Hokkien for bad luck) if one's feet accidentally gets swept or touched by the broom. The colour black, the dominant colour in Halloween decorations, is frowned upon by the Chinese as it symbolises death. But then, this was not Chinese New Year, this was Halloween.

Halloween was an ancient celebration with its origins in the Catholic Church. It comes from a contracted corruption of All Hallows Eve. The 1st of November or All Hallows Day (or All Saints' Day) is a Catholic day of observance in honour of saints. One myth goes that the disembodied spirits of the dead in the past year would come back in search of live bodies to possess for the coming year, the only hope of an afterlife.

Naturally, the living did not wish to be possessed and so on the 31st of October, the villagers would dress up in all manner of scary, ghoulish costumes and parade noisily around the neighbourhood in the hope of frightening away the evil spirits. With time, the belief in possession by spirits waned and the custom of dressing up as hobgoblins, demons, ghosts, witches took on a more ceremonial role. The custom of Halloween was brought over to America by the Irish immigrants during the Potato famine of Ireland in the 1840s.

Thus, Halloween was a celebration of good against evil, of light over the dark forces, it certainly wasn't demon worship. I felt that the school authorities should have stuck to their guns and stood up against this kind of paranoia. It is implausible to be too PC all the time, and to try and please all the different communities in multicultural America. Just goes to show that in trying not to offend some of the people some of the time, one ends up offending all the people all the time.

Red Injuns and
Other Unspeakables

When the British empire faded into the pages of history, they left behind in their former colonies a legacy of sorts ranging from the English language, their systems of administration and education, English names, the English cuppa, cricket, and a love for English football. I was educated in an English medium school, and my education throughout primary and secondary school was very Anglocentric in content. I learnt quite a number of British folk songs, ballads, and chants. At twelve years of age, I could sing Scottish ballads such as 'Loch Lomond', 'Annie Laurie', 'Bonnie Charlie', 'Coming Through the Rye', Irish songs such as 'Londonderry Air', 'When Irish Eyes are Smiling' and English songs such as 'Lili Marlene' and 'Scarborough Fair'. I also had a repertoire of chants in my childhood, some of which were in English.

One English chant that should have disappeared with the Empire was a little verse that we children used to sing whenever we had to decide who would be 'It' in our games. The chant was the Eeeny Meeny Miny Moe chant, and it went like this:

Eeeny Meeny Miny Moe
Catch a nigger by his toe
If he dies, you shall cry
Eeeny Meeny Miny Moe

It was just a chant, not Shakespeare, and we never for a minute thought about its contents, nor analysed it. We intoned it when the occasion arose, innocently, in cheerful nonchalance as we pointed to each other, turn by turn with each syllable of the chant and when the chant ended, the person being pointed to would be 'It'. How were we to know in those innocent days that there would eventually be something called PC or political correctness? How would we have even guessed that this relic from the days of the Empire would one day come to haunt us?

And so it did one day in Texas when I was at the park at a get-together of Malaysian expatriate families based in Houston (there is quite a large number of Malaysians, mostly based in the oil and gas industry). While the adults chatted and picnicked in the shade of the trees, the children were happily playing all sorts of games in the park.

Then I heard the old chant which I hadn't heard since my childhood. I pricked up my ears ... I couldn't believe what I heard! A group of children were happily chanting away the Eeeny Meeny Miny Moe song, replete with mention of the 'N' word, for their game of Hide and Seek.

"Urrrpppp," I gasped.

I clamped my mouth with horror as if it would sub-consciously clamp up those kids' big mouths too. I looked around furtively and was unnerved to see some Americans around, as a number had been invited to the gathering. Some were spouses of Malaysian expats. Fortunately, there weren't any African Americans there that day. The word 'nigger' is offensive to the African Americans as it has derogatory and racist connotations and was used to refer to the blacks when they were slaves in the US. To make things worse, just recently in the news, two roughnecks in some boondocks of Texas, had caught a poor harmless black man, tied him up by his feet to the back of their truck and driven the truck around in a mad frenzy of racist hatred and sheer thuggery, and killed the poor hapless victim. Now was certainly not the right time to recite that ludicrous dated chant.

I looked at the Malaysian parents around me—they seemed to be enjoying themselves, doing the thing that Malaysians do best, eating. They were tucking away at the wonderful array of food which the women had cooked and brought along to the park, oblivious to the boo-boo just committed on American soil. I looked at the children—they were totally innocent and did not realise that here in America, especially in the Deep South, you just do not use that word 'nigger', nor anywhere else in the US, for that matter.

I had to do a fix-it. Why me? I groaned. Why do I have to notice such things? Was it because I specialise in the English language? I felt like the kid in the movie *The Sixth Sense*—the little boy who could see ghosts and spirits, except that my problem was far more mundane—I could hear the ghosts of the former British empire—linguistic relics still floating around in former British colonies, which had not hooked into the PC (political correctness) nor the feminist movements unlike in the English native-speaker countries where PC had emerged as a strong force.

"Eeny meeny miny moe …"

There they go again … "Shuuussshhhhh …" I hissed, like a witch from a crazy fairy tale, at the children.

I hated being the nosey parker and they weren't my kids but I knew that something had to be done. I hurried stealthily over to them, placing a finger over my lips, glancing all around me as if we were in some magic forest, and the demons or *toyols* (small mythical creatures) would get us. I whispered to the children that the chant they were singing was not very nice—rather rude, in fact. I suggested a popular Malaysian chant—the '*La li lah tum pong*' chant instead. They stared at me as if I were some weird busybody still undergoing childhood or perhaps commencing her second one.

"What's with this kinky lady? Why can't she be an adult and eat like what the rest of the adults are doing and let us children play and be ourselves?" I can see the accusation in their eyes.

"Er … Aunty, we don't know the '*La li lah tum pong*' chant-lah!"

"Oh …" I smiled sheepishly at them. During my childhood days, we used it all the time to decide who would be 'It'. Well yes, my childhood did take place some time ago but I didn't think the chant had gone out of fashion that quickly.

"Okay, okay. Use the word 'Tiger' then, not the 'N' word, okay?" I suggested. "Catch a tiger by its toe, okay?"

The children looked at me, all wide-eyed and disbelieving, and nodded.

Thank goodness there weren't any 'Love the Tiger' group members or environmental activists here, I thought … I'll worry about that one later.

The get-together eventually drew to an end. We had feasted on some favourites of Malaysian cuisine like *rendang*, *satay*, *popiah*, *mee soto*, *lontong*, fried *mee hoon*, *mee siam*, and enjoyed catching up with the Malaysian expat crowd, I was rolling up my picnic mat and minding my own business when two Malaysian

women acquaintances, the wives of Malaysian expats working in Houston, came strolling by. One was boasting loudly about her travels in the US.

"Oh, we've been to so many places, we've travelled all over the US. We've done New Orleans, San Francisco, Disneyland!" she gushed.

She continued name-dropping a load of places and destinations.

"We've been to New York, Boston, Hawaii, Alabama. Last summer, we went to Los Angeles, Las Vegas. We also did Florida. Next month, we are going to New Mexico," she continued.

"Wahh, it seems there-ah got Red Injuns one, you know," she said in a hushed, excited voice.

"Huh? Really-ah? Still got Red Indians-ah? Aiyohh, wah, so scary-eh," exclaimed the other.

For a moment, I couldn't believe my ears again, but sure enough, here was another relic of the old empire. Red Injuns or Red Indians—surely these words couldn't still be around to describe the Native Americans, but yes, here they were, still being used by these two Malaysian women. Not so bad as 'nigger' but for heaven's sake, still using 'Red Injuns' in this day and age?

I cringed … don't tell me I have to open my big mouth again …

Speaking with Different Tongues

The other day in a discussion group at a Graduate class at the University, I was annoyed at how 'insular' a bunch of Americans were. They were mainly Anglo-American school teachers. They lamented how these Asian learners of English "just can't get their sounds right." I was particularly incensed at the American professor teaching the particular class who should have known better. Instead, she reinforced their views and commented, "Yeah, they just don't get it. I tell my ESL students to say 'Fried Rice' and they say, 'Yeah, that's what I said, Flied Lice'!" Some members of the group sniggered.

I was bothered by that comment, particularly at the sniggering. I couldn't let it go just like that. I had to point out that it wasn't because of the stupidity of the Asians, but that their tongues were unfamiliar with the sound 'r' as it does not exist in their language.

I piped up, "You know, one can put the shoe on the other foot too. You guys can't pronounce a lot of sounds that exist in other languages as well. For example, many of you can't pronounce a common Chinese surname 'Ng'. It's all to do with the tongue and its familiarity with certain sounds."

I had a number of Malaysian friends there with the surname 'Ng' who ended up being called Angie because the Americans can't enunciate the sound 'Ng'. Likewise, Chinese names like 'Kam' which should be pronounced 'Kum' end up as 'Kamp'. If you have the name of 'Kuen', don't even try—you will probably end up being called Queen or Kim. My friend Hon Ming, who lives in the US, was forced to take on the English name of Michael because he got fed up with people calling him 'Horny'. Another friend on an international assignment to Dallas changed his name Chir Sing to an English one, 'Chris' as they could not enunciate his Chinese name but called him 'Chasing' and 'Cheers' instead. My cousin, Loong, a doctor, also had to take on a Western name, Chris, because they couldn't pronounce his Chinese name. If only the Americans knew how many of us have had to change our Chinese names and take on American ones, not because we are smitten with these 'Christian' names but simply because we can't bear the daily mutilation of our Chinese names, I thought.

What I was trying to convey to the group really was that it wasn't so pat and simple—not being able to pronounce certain words in English for certain cultural groups could be because of the influence of their native languages. Different peoples have different phonological systems in their language and if one group has problems pronouncing the words of another language, it was merely because of our diversity and differences, not stupidity!

The American woman professor glared at me. I could sense her wrath for trying to show her up. I must have been an annoyance because I did not conform to the stereotype of the quiet, reticent Asian student. I participated actively in class (speaking out frequently), and asked questions which many

Asian students seldom did. I made friends with people as people, and refused to cling to just the 'safety' of Asian friends. I could speak and write in perfect English and here I was challenging them and even telling them about how our tongues and brains were wired!

Fortunately or unfortunately for me, the president of the US during my time there was President Bill Clinton. George W. Bush had not become president yet, otherwise it might have helped my case further if I had told the naïve professor that the president of the most powerful country on earth cannot pronounce the word 'Nuclear'. And that was in the English language.

To my surprise (not really anymore, actually), instead of an ensuing discussion in class, they just listened stumped, as if it couldn't even sink in, and then changed the subject altogether. It would have been interesting to pursue the discussion further. But that was it—end of discussion. No one wanted to go to down that unknown road any farther. Perhaps for fear that one's ethnocentricity would show up …

I wanted to say, "Hey c'mon, ask me questions … open your minds … don't you want to know more about what I'm trying to share with you? The rest of the world knows so much about America … at least be a little interested in the rest of the world."

The class continued in its little safe ethnocentric journey.

I met up with some friends for dinner after that and shared what had happened in class. Marti, an acquaintance who had lived in the US for the past three years, was irate, nodding her head, wanting to say something.

She finally burst out, "Hey, you think that's bad. The other day at a party, I was asked by some Americans where I learnt to speak English. And this was after I told them that I come from Australia!"

Decisions ... Decisions ...

America has often been called the Land of the Rich and Plenty. I certainly wouldn't disagree with that, especially the 'Plenty' part. One thing that delighted as well as exasperated me about living in the US was the incredible array of choices available. Americans are the world's greatest consumerists. Indeed, consumerism is a religion here.

Every morning, especially on weekends, my mailbox at home was stuffed with flyers exhorting one to shop, buy, transact and spend, spend, spend! There were flyers on everything ranging from cosmetics to household appliances to property. There were flyers from clubs and gyms urging you to join, flyers from the big department stores such as Foley's, Macy's and Wal-Mart urging you to shop, flyers from the big supermarkets such as Albertsons, Randalls, Fiesta, urging you to buy their goods on special offer, flyers from factory outlet malls urging you to binge on incredible bargains. Apart from flyers, the mailbox was stuffed with catalogues from fashion houses, subscription orders, mail orders, online forms, advertorials from insurance agents, and wads of coupons.

The coupon culture is unbelievable, and a terrible wastage

of paper. Intelligent capable individuals are reduced to fastidious nitpicky coupon-counting, coupon-calculating humanoids. As if plastic and cash are not currency enough, in the US, you can accrue so-called incredible savings by using coupons which entitle you to some kind of discounts on goods and services. Some Malaysian expat wives there swear they get to save ten to twenty percent of their monthly expenditure by using coupons.

I found it a waste of time. On my first few attempts at playing this coupon game, I found that I could never get my timing of coupon usage and my visits to the supermarkets right. When I finally managed to pull out a coupon at the right place, it was the wrong time—the coupon had expired. When I got the right time, it was the wrong place. I finally ignored the whole coupon consumerist culture. Besides, there is this truism that there is no free lunch. One can bet that there is always a catch—by enticing you there to use the coupon, you end up spending on other things using money you think you have so ingeniously saved. Even if it worked somewhat, it is an appalling waste of paper—how can the US preach to others to conserve their rainforests and not cut down trees? What about the LAYOB principle?? Look at Your Own Backyard first—look at the horrendous amount of paper that is being consumed before pointing at the massacre of trees in other peoples' countries. Without this voracious demand for paper, there wouldn't be such a supply.

Coming back to the Land of Plenty, the choices are just bewildering. Take for instance a simple foray into a famous fried chicken outlet.

After placing an order of chicken, the waiter asks, "What side dish would you like, Mam?"

I was puzzled initially because in Malaysia you don't get

choices—all you get is a little bun and a dollop of coleslaw. Here, you have to decide whether you want macaroni, coleslaw, mashed potatoes, potato wedges, Spanish rice, corn bread, buns, fried onion rings, potato rings, baked beans, the list goes on …

At a restaurant, even when ordering a simple salad, the choices of salad dressings are amazing.

"And what kind of salad dressing would you like, Mam?"

"What do you have?"

"Well, we have French, Italian, Ranch, Thousand Island …"

As if this didn't make one's life hard enough, try breakfast at IHOP or the International House of Pancakes. A simple order of a pancake or two is too simple in the life of an American—one must make choices and decisions yet again.

"What kind of syrup would you like, Mam? We have maple, chocolate, blueberry, honey, and cranberry syrup."

If syrup coating one's pancake wasn't enough, you also have a choice of whether you want to smother your nice fluffy pancake with toppings—chocolate fudge topping, strawberry topping, blueberry topping, cranberry topping, and if you like, whipped cream too!

It was hard to resist—the choices were just so tempting. For someone used to a simple cup of coffee and a slice of toast for breakfast, I would stagger out of IHOP bloated and about to burst.

Choices don't just happen in 'happy' places—they also happen in 'stressful' places—such as at the dentist's. When I took my son for his dental check-up, after examining Jan Ming's teeth, the dentist asked him a strange question.

"Well, young man, and what will it be today?"

Jan Ming went, "Huh?"

I agreed too—I mean … du-uuhhhh … this was the

dentist's. What could possibly take place here other than extreme pain and torture?

The dentist explained, "What kind of teeth polish would you like?"

"Er what did you say ? You mean … you mean to say there are actually choices in polishing teeth?" I asked, stupefied.

"Oh yes, strawberry, chocolate, mint, raspberry, blueberry, peppermint … et cetera, et cetera."

Jan Ming's face broke into a happy toothless smile. "STRAWBERRY!" he said happily.

Even when my son fractured his arm swinging on the monkey bars in school, there were choices to be made after the kind doctor had put his arm in a plaster cast. The American Iranian doctor took out a chart containing little colourful squares and asked Jan Ming to choose a colour for the bandage wrapping his plaster cast. Jan Ming could not decide between a bright turquoise and bright purple. For awhile, we got so wrapped up trying to decide on a colour, we quite forgot the boy had just broken his arm on the monkey bars.

Finally, the plucky rascal grinned and yelled, "PURPLE!" I winced. Uggh! I hate purple. I would have preferred peach or mauve instead but then, sigh … alas … it wasn't my arm in the cast.

Step into a supermarket and the choices are simply staggering. All kinds of coffees from all parts of the world, biscuits lining an entire row of shelves, snacks and crispies filling another two rows, an entire section just devoted to breads, pastries and sweets and confectionery. The choices of cheeses left me dumbfounded—before this trip to the US all I knew of cheese was the paper thin ones wrapped in plastic. I found I took much more time in the big supermarts because I had to pause

to decide all the time when confronted with numerous choices. At the end of one's 'ordeal', as one reaches the cashier, there's one more decision to make!

"Paper or Plastic?" the cashier asks you. Aaarrggghhh.

I remember that embarrassing time when I had to buy some sanitary towels. I was in a big hurry that morning. I had to rush to campus to attend a lecture. The nearest store was this huge Albertsons supermarket. I trudged along the aisles ignoring all those enticing rows of things to buy and headed straight for the toiletries section. When I finally reached the women's toiletry section, my heart sank. There was an entire row of boxes and packets of sanitary towels—thick ones, thin ones, fat ones, slim ones, long-haul, short-haul, wingless, winged, looped, unlooped, hooked, unhooked, mild days, heavy days, dribble days, bad bloody days, pouring-by-the-bucket days, thin elegant wafers, thick bleeding-to-death ones … what was a woman to do? Sigh … decisions, decisions. I just didn't have the luxury of time to browse.

What's wrong with these Americans? I thought. Why can't life be a bit more simple? Who on earth has the time to read all these labels? Grumpily, I grabbed one without bothering to read—I reckon they all had one same function anyway.

I learnt a lesson that day. I put one on in a rush in the Ladies before dashing madly to Research Methods class. Throughout class, I found myself see-sawing on my wooden chair. It was getting really hard to concentrate on the wonders of Quantitative Research when I was trying to research why my bum wasn't exactly in total contact with the wooden surface of my chair. I was sitting on a thick wad of cotton, so stuffed I was hovering above my chair. On checking it out later, I found that, drat, in my haste, I had grabbed a pack of giant-sized pads for old people suffering from incontinence!

Little Vietnam

An interesting find I made during my stay in Houston was an ethnic enclave in the Bellaire area, which I called Little Vietnam. One could buy fresh seafood and vegetables in the supermarkets there and patronise the abundant Vietnamese cafes and restaurants. Whenever I missed my favourite Malaysian hawker fare *char koay teow*, I would head for Little Vietnam where I could buy the softest smoothest *koay teow* from a Vietnamese woman selling all types of noodles and soybean products freshly made in the morning.

I loved Vietnamese food—its flavours, the abundance of herbs and vegetables such as basil, beans and bean sprouts accompanying the noodle and soup dishes were simply delicious. Being a coffee lover, my first taste of Vietnamese coffee sent me over the moon—so strong and pungent and thick one could cut one's teeth on it. Some of my favourite dishes were the prawns wrapped around sugar cane sticks, the paper-thin Vietnamese spring rolls, the scrumptious prawn balls and the interesting noodle dishes. Whenever I was too lazy to cook, when I got bored with American seafood coated in bread crumbs and fried to a boring blandness, when I longed for light fresh wholesome food, it was to Little Vietnam that I would happily retreat to.

My favourite hairstylist was a fair and lovely young Vietnamese lady who worked in a hair salon in Little Vietnam. Her name was Penny, I never found out her Vietnamese name. She had light brown eyes and pan-Asian looks. Once, I asked her about her hazel-brown eyes; she mentioned that somewhere in her past, there was a French connection, most likely between her grandmother and a Frenchman but her parents and grandparents would not tell her much.

In Penny's comfortable hair salon, with Vietnamese music playing in the background, I would watch, in fascination through the salon mirrors, the Vietnamese hair-stylists and shampoo girls working there. They were all young, slim and good-looking, and fluent in their mother tongue. Their customers were mostly Vietnamese but when an American customer stepped in, they would code-switch into broken American English, adequate enough to keep the customer happy.

I remember the TV images of the Americans beating a hasty retreat from Vietnam when the Vietcong defeated the South Vietnamese in 1975: throngs of desperate Vietnamese mobbing the American embassy, climbing, clawing their way up to the rooftop of the embassy, jousting for a place on the few remaining helicopters, begging for escape from the impending horrors that would be unleashed by the enemy. I wondered about the stories of the escape from Vietnam from the Vietnamese side as all the stories I had heard so far were from the American side or from American movies. I wondered if some of these young ladies in their tight jeans strutting about in the salon were the products of those frenzied moments—how many of them were those little babies that desperate mothers thrust into the arms of the American soldiers?

Curious, I asked Penny how she came to America. Penny said she was only five years old when her parents escaped from Vietnam, and she could not remember much. Her parents had connections with the Americans and were given safe passage out of Saigon before its fall in 1975. Once every two years, Penny would return to Vietnam to visit relatives there. Many people there still live in abject poverty. Everyone she knew had lost someone or entire families in the Vietnam War.

Once when I commented on a beautifully poignant Vietnamese melody being played on her CD player, Penny replied wistfully, "The story of Vietnam is always about sadness. That is why all the songs that you hear from the Vietnamese are sad songs, there are no happy songs."

Somehow, that remark is indelibly stuck in my head.

My first encounter with the Vietnamese tragedy occurred more than twenty years ago. It was 1978 and I was holidaying with my mother in a luxury hotel in Kuantan, a town on the east coast of Peninsular Malaysia. The late seventies up to the mid-eighties was the height of the exodus of the Boat People from Vietnam. South Vietnam had fallen to the communists in 1975, but many South Vietnamese were still desperately trying to escape by boat, taking terrible risks with their lives as they set out on overcrowded rickety boats, pointing their vessels southwards or westwards in the hope of reaching friendly countries who would take them in.

I still remember that Sunday morning vividly. My mother and I were sitting on deck chairs looking out to sea, enjoying the gentle sea breeze, and a beautiful sunny morning. I was reading a book while my mother was enjoying her favourite past-time, i.e. people watching. There were some people bathing in the sea, a few children were nonchalantly building sandcastles, several teenagers were squealing happily as the waves from the South China Sea came rolling onto the shore. It was just an ordinary day by the sea.

Then, a strange brown speck appeared on the horizon to a distant puttering sound. It was moving so slowly along it looked like it was on its last legs. No one took much notice of it at first, but as the object chugged slowly nearer and nearer into view, people stopped doing whatever they were doing and stared at the approaching object. It was a ramshackle, decrepit boat that had seen harrowing times at sea. It looked as if it were about to collapse from its journey. There were some clothes, more like rags, hanging out to dry on the boat. It was obvious it was not a fishing vessel, nor a cruise boat of tourists.

"*Orang Vietnam! Orang Vietnam!*" ("Vietnamese people!" in Malay) I heard some locals shouting.

People were beginning to run towards the shoreline. I could not discern whether there were expressions of anger or curiosity or welcoming looks on their faces, as they rushed down the beach towards where the boat was approaching. Then, suddenly the puttering stopped. Someone on board the boat had stopped the engine, it was now floating about two hundred metres from the shore. The draught of the boat was very low suggesting a heavy burden on board, yet oddly, it seemed that there were only three men on board. They were standing on the deck of the boat, staring curiously at us, just as we were staring incredulously at them. They seemed uneasy and uncertain, as if overjoyed to hit land yet fearful of its inhabitants.

The breeze grew stronger. The waves were forming into huge swells and the boat drifted broadside. A huge wave tossed the boat upwards. For a moment, the little boat was poised precariously, suspended on the frothing crest of an enormous wave. We heard terrified screams of women and children from the boat. The wave rolled away from under the boat. The creaky vessel miraculously managed to stay afloat. We could hear muffled screams and cries and we realised there must have been around twenty to thirty people on board! They were hiding inside, unsure of how they would be received, probably lost as to where they were.

One man from the boat dived into the sea and swam to shore. Some hotel officials met him and gesticulated to him to take the boat to another beach nearby, where there was probably a safe landing house for the Vietnamese boat people. He swam back to the rickety boat, started the engine and the dilapidated vessel chugged slowly out of sight, heading towards a promontory of the bay.

I never saw the other passengers of that boat. I was amazed at their discipline, staying hidden despite sighting land and obeying the orders of their leaders, or perhaps they were weak from hunger, thirst and the elements. Who knows what horrors had befallen them on their perilous journey across the seas. There had been horrifying news reports of pirates preying on these hapless refugees stripping them of their gold and possessions, raping the women, murdering and tossing the men and children overboard. All I could remember were the piercing screams of the women and children on that brave little boat, haunting me for a long time.

A year later, my path crossed with the Vietnamese Boat people, again from a distance. In my first job—in 1979—at a local university in Bangi, I had to drive along the Kuala Lumpur-Seremban Highway to get to work ... The Red Cross had built a camp at Sungei Besi just beside the highway. This camp was one of the transit camps for the refugees from the island of

Pulau Bidong off the east coast of Trengganu, a state in north-eastern Peninsular Malaysia, where thousands of boat people were living temporarily. After screening by the authorities, the selected refugees were brought to the Sungei Besi camp where they were eventually flown to various countries who had agreed to accept them. Malaysia would not open its doors to the Boat People for fear of social problems but agreed to let them use one of its uninhabited islands, Pulau Bidong as a refugee camp, while the International Red Cross and other humanitarian concerns worked hard to find homes for them.

I passed by the Sungei Besi camp every morning. The refugees were confined to the camp premises, surrounded by a high wall with barbed wire. They could not come out, and no one without official permission could get in. This time they didn't stay hidden but perched on the balcony of the top floor of the two-storey wooden barracks, peering out at the cars whizzing by. They looked thin, wiry and dark from exposure to the sun. Every day, I would see a number of them hanging around on that balcony, looking longingly at the outside world. Day in day out, their view of the world was one of hundreds of vehicles whizzing by on that busy highway, their drivers intent on reaching their destinations, the scenery a bleak highway landscape without many trees. I noticed there were little children in the camp too, and sometimes women carrying babies in their arms, probably born while in detention.

After several years they were more or less forgotten or totally ignored, just another landmark on the bland Sungei Besi landscape. Many batches of Boat People must have lived there for awhile before moving on to designated countries. After 4 or 5 years, the 'dregs' were left behind—I suppose they must have been confined there for a long time because one morning, as I drove past the camp, I was surprised to see some frenzied activity going on in the camp. The inhabitants were standing on the top storey and balconies of the barracks, holding up banners beseeching to be let out of the camps, begging for haste in their applications for political asylum. They waved at us drivers as we drove by, shouting, shaking their fists and pointing frantically at their banners. The next day, when I drove by, I saw that the barracks had been gutted. The refugees had set fire to the building, venting their frustration and rage. They were moved to another camp elsewhere and I never saw them again.

The next time my paths crossed with the Vietnamese was here in Houston where many of the boat people had been repatriated two decades ago. They were doing well from the little I know of my interactions with them at Bellaire, they must have gone through terrible times which they don't want to talk about; a new generation of Vietnamese had sprung up, many of whom were highly adaptive and successful in their new adopted homeland, and they were free, if not of the ghosts and a tragic past, they were finally free to live their lives without anymore fear and terror, and free to achieve their dreams and aspirations.

Boat People Encounters

They drift
Like unwanted debris
Flotsam pieces
On cold hostile
Deadly blue waters
Packed into boats
Hoping

They hang
Like lifeless creatures
Human slow lorises
On rough makeshift
Sticks and stilts
Packed into barracks
Waiting

The world does not want them
Reminders of an ugly mindless war
Yet they hope and wait
For a day
When they can sing again
And play their music
Always, always
That sad sad music …

By Lee Su Kim

Affirm Me?
Thanks but No Thanks

It was intriguing to come over to the US and find myself qualifying for three categories of peoples that get to enjoy special privileges. It's called affirmative action here. The three categories are: Language minorities, Ethnic minorities and Women. I could understand the existence of the first two but the third category was rather a surprise to me. Women—a disadvantaged group? In many countries in Asia, there are women who face tougher challenges than men because of gender discrimination and male chauvinism, but it was surprising to learn that in the US, women still face discrimination in the job market.

In Malaysia, there are affirmative action policies in place, with the objective of helping the Malays, albeit the majority race, to catch up economically with the Chinese, a large minority in the country, who are mainly in the urban areas and regarded as a wealthy and economically powerful group. Affirmative action would and indeed has, to an extent, helped to lessen the cleavage between the Malays and the Chinese, and create an educated and well-off Malay middle class as well as a class of Malay millionaires. Here in the US though, it is the minorities that need some kind of assistance and affirmative action was introduced to help balance the imbalance in the distribution of wealth and opportunities.

Having never been on the receiving end of affirmative action policies in my homeland, it therefore came as a surprise to me when my Academic Advisor at the university, an American professor, proudly told me that I could apply for scholarships or awards for people from the three disadvantaged groups. After all, I qualified, being an Asian, a Malaysian Chinese and a woman. I was surprised by my own reaction—I found myself rejecting any kind of assistance.

"No thanks," I said firmly. "I want to know that if I win anything or am awarded anything, it is on my own merit. Nothing to do with my gender, colour or ethnicity."

"But Su Kim, if there are opportunities here, why not?" asked the professor curiously.

He was surprised at my response. He thought that many of 'us' would like to 'ride' on the affirmative action policies here in the US.

"It is more a question of 'Why?' rather than 'Why not?' Why do I need affirmative action?" I responded, "I don't need affirmation. I need confirmation."

What I seek more is the truth—I need to know where I stand in relation to the others. I am curious to know whether my education and experience have equipped me to compete amongst people from all over the world. What better place to find out than here in the US? If I win anything, is it because I deserve it, or is it because of my LEG (language/ethnicity/gender)? I want to play on an equal playing field like everyone else, I don't want the goal post moved a little nearer for me. Just the same-sized bat like all the other American graduate students will do, thank you, not a bigger one to hit the ball. I am sure there are many in the

US who may have come from underprivileged backgrounds or poverty-stricken situations who need a boost along the way, but I certainly do not feel that being a woman is disadvantageous, or that being an Asian woman from a developing country is some kind of blot against me.

Thus, the only affirmation I need is through my own efforts. I need to know that if I win any awards or score distinctions along the way, it's based on my merit and performance, not because I represent three deprived categories. I do not desire any 'special privileges', just fairness and impartiality regardless of what sex, colour or creed I am.

(At the end of the doctoral programme, I scored twenty distinctions in all the twenty courses I had enrolled for. I was also awarded a distinction for my doctoral dissertation. My CGPA—Cumulative grade point average—was a perfect four. I took four years altogether from start to finish. It had been extremely tough and stressful at times, but at the end of the day, it felt really good to know that it was all on my own steam.)

Pulled Tea?

Before I left the shores of Malaysia, I went on a crazy shopping spree on the eve of my departure—rushing around the hypermarket tossing packets of instant noodles, curry powders, spices, *belachan* cubes, *tom yam* paste, bottles of thick black Cheong Chan soy sauce and Ghee Hiang sesame oil, *ketupat* and *rendang* mixes, as well as *assam pedas* and *assam tumis* mixes into my shopping trolley. You name them—I had them! The ultimate *kiasu* ('afraid of losing' in Hokkien) expat. I was prepared. I wasn't going to spend my days howling at the moon in Texas longing for *sambal belachan* or chilli sauce. If I should miss Malaysian food, I could always cook it over there, I thought.

Well, I felt really sheepish after I arrived in Houston. I found out that here, you can get almost anything and that my worries had been in vain. Apart from an excellent range of supplies in supermarkets such as the Fiesta chain of supermarkets, there was a Chinatown and a 'Little Vietnam' in Bellaire, and a 'Little India' in the Hillcroft area. In these ethnic ghettoes, one can find supermarkets and shops selling everything one desires.

But then, when you are far away from home, it is amazing to find that what you miss most are the simplest and most

ordinary things. I found myself missing the humble *teh tarik*.
Teh tarik, if you don't know already, is a very popular drink with
all Malaysians. It is thick, strong tea with a wonderful frothy
layer, somewhat like a café latte. The more foam at the top, the
better. It is sold mainly at the ubiquitous Mamak (slang for
Indian Muslim) shops and stalls in Malaysia. It literally means
'pulled tea' in Malay.

I just couldn't find *teh tarik* anywhere in Texas. There were
no Malaysian restaurants in Houston when I was there and you
certainly can't buy it at Starbucks or McDonald's. I sought out
the Indian restaurants in Hillcroft but the closest they could
aspire to in response to my persistent enquiries was Indian
Ginger Tea. I even tried to describe the recipe to them so that
someone could come up with something similar.

"*Teh tarik*? You know *teh tarik* … it means pulled tea. You've
got to pull it, you know … pull it far apart. Er, vertically of
course … then join it again … you know … st-r-e-t-c-h it," I
tried to explain desperately to the waiter at an Indian restaurant
in Houston.

"Mam, do you want *masala* tea, Mam? We do not have *tea
tareeq*," answers he, thinking I must be either quite mad or stark
pregnant.

"No, no, I don't want your *masala* tea. I want my *teh tarik*.
Tea that has been pulled. It can be any kind of tea but just pull
it. PULL IT, you hear, and you get *teh tarik*."

It was exasperating. Somehow, the concept of pulling a
liquid is totally alien to these guys. I am convinced that if only
someone had bothered to listen to my ranting and learnt how
to make this wonderful Malaysian-originated tea, he would be
a rich man today with an entire franchise of *teh tarik* tea shops
throughout the US.

Then a divine idea hit me one day as I stared out grumpily at a beautiful bright blue Texan morning, missing my cuppa. DIY! Why didn't I think of it earlier? I could DO-IT-YOURSELF! So I cheerily put the kettle on the stove and made myself a pot of tea. I tasted it but it didn't feel quite right. Rather too high class a tea bag, I thought. My Uncle Foo once told me, in an effort to make me more health-conscious, that the Mamaks use cheap tea dust for their *teh tarik*. Alas, my expensive Earl Grey Organic Tea with the Queen of England's seal couldn't quite pass the test. Aaahhh but I haven't pulled it yet, I whispered excitedly to myself.

I poured the tea into a jug. With a glass in one hand and the jug in the other, I went to the kitchen sink and pulled and stretched the tea like crazy. I felt extremely vertically challenged. My arm span wasn't long enough to give it that length and height and complexity. The aroma was missing too.

Froth, you stupid tea, c'mon, start frothing.

I tried to visualise the Mamak at my favourite coffee shop back home in Petaling Jaya. Such style he had, such amazing technique. Most of my *teh tarik* spilled into the sink. The more frothiness I desired, the less tea I collected. In the end, after all the pulling and stretching, I had only about two and half inches of a very unhappy-looking, dishevelled tea in a glass with sticky stained sides and where the &*!#* is the foam?

The Lonesome Durian

*When God designed the durian, he definitely had in mind the
spirit of friendship and camaraderie that has to be shared when
partaking of this remarkable fruit. Ever come across anyone
eating the durian all by himself? That would be the epitome of
loneliness.*

*Lee Su Kim, columnist,
on the right ambience for enjoying certain things to the fullest.*

On 1 September 1994, I had the singular privilege of 'rubbing
shoulders' with a number of VIPs—politicians, bankers,
CEOs and other famous personalities. This was because I
was quoted together with the rest in a column entitled 'Duly
Noted'—a compilation of quotes from various local Malaysian
personalities—in a local magazine devoted to the Malaysian
business community. The quote attributed to me was taken
from my own column in a leading English language national
newspaper, *The Star*.

   I found myself in select company with people like Dr.
Mahathir—the Prime Minister of Malaysia at that time, Rashid

Hussain—a high-flying stockbroker, Lee Lam Thye—a human rights activist, Claude Le Roy—the Atlanta Olympics soccer coach, etc. The preamble to the column 'Duly Noted' stated this: "We present below slices of verbal Malaysiana; the witty and pungent coexisting, like all things national, with the trite and inane." And there, to my utmost surprise was a quote from me on my views about the durian.

Me! Being quoted in a business journal? I couldn't believe my eyes. While there were snippets quoting the PM on high finance and CEOs on business practices, I was being quoted on the sacred topic of the durian. I'm not sure whose words were considered inane, trite or witty but I would certainly vouch that mine must have qualified for the most pungent.

Anyway, coming back to the content of the quote, I would like to counter my earlier claim here in this book. I was wrong in 1994. Eating the durian all by oneself in one's homeland is NOT the epitome of loneliness. Eating the durian all by oneself far away in a foreign land is even more earth-shattering and is the true epitome of loneliness.

I say this based on my experience with the durian in Texas. After a year and a half in the US, I was beginning to miss some things terribly, one of which was the durian. The durian is an extremely popular Malaysian fruit, and in fact is considered the King of Fruits. If you are a Malaysian (or if you are from Indonesia or Thailand) there is no need for any explanation. But if you are not, the durian is a spiny, thorny football-sized fruit with the most divine smell. Most Southeast Asians would think so. However, for those who hate it, the smell of the durian has been described as the smell of rotting flesh, or eating odoriferous squelchy custard in a toilet. The smell of the durian is so strong and pungent that it is banned in hotels and on aeroplanes. The French naturalist, Henri Mouhot describes it this way: "On first tasting it, I thought it like the flesh of some animal in a state of putrefaction." The 19th-century American journalist Baynard Taylor wrote that, "To eat it seems to be the sacrifice of self-respect."

The durian is extremely hard to open as it is covered with sharp thorns (*duri* in Malay) and an innocent walk in a durian orchard or the forest can kill you if a durian should fall on your head! Hellish on the outside, it is heaven on the inside—the rich custardy bittersweet flavours of the gorgeous golden-yellow flesh of the durian has transported many a durian lover to Paradise. You cannot sit on the fence with the durian—you either love it or hate it.

I knew it would be hopeless to look for durians in the American supermarkets. But I was told that occasionally, you could find them in the Chinese supermarkets, in the freezer section. One day after prodding the ice in a huge freezer in a Chinese supermarket in Bellaire, Houston, wonder of wonders, I saw a yellow-greenish thorny fruit emerge. It was a durian! I poked further, impatiently pushing the ice shavings away and behold, there were two more half-buried there.

Now to go about selecting my durian. I hauled one up from its bed of ice and sniffed it. There was no smell. It was so frozen it had lost its smell. Imagine a durian without an aroma—that was almost like castrating the poor fruit! Still, I was determined to take at least one home. If odour could not help, perhaps appearance could. I looked at its colour, the shape of its thorns—it looked pathetic, having spent months buried in the freezer, thousands of miles away from its native land.

By now, a small crowd of curious Chinese onlookers had gathered around. They were probably from Taiwan or China, living in the US, and were not familiar with the tropical fruit. They stared curiously as I pulled out one durian after another.

"What is this thing called?" a Chinese man asked me.

"Durian. It's called a durian!" I said earnestly.

"Does it taste good?"

"What? Does it taste good? Does the sun shine? Is the sky blue? A durian is just divine. It is absolutely delicious. Its smell is fabulous. In my country, it is the King of Fruits," I raved.

"What smell?" he asked as he sniffed one gingerly.

A few other curious onlookers were by now also prodding and sniffing the other durians in the ice.

"What smell?" another woman asked.

"Yeah," I agreed, "What smell?? It's been frozen for too long. It has lost its smell. It usually smells like a slice of heaven."

Unimpressed, the few curious onlookers drifted away.

I hauled up one durian after another, sniffing and shaking them only to wrinkle my nose with disgust at the odourless pathetic sods. Finally, I grabbed one durian by the stalk and headed for the cashier, determined not to let the scentless durians deter me from buying one.

I took home my precious durian and placed it on the kitchen counter. The house where we lived in was a beautiful, large two-storey home in the suburbs, fully carpeted and air-conditioned with central heating. Everything had been done up in white by the landlord, from the carpets to the curtains to the kitchen cabinets. There, in the dazzling whiteness of my American home, with all the windows and doors closed, I sat patiently waiting for my forlorn exotic friend, still with chips of ice stuck amidst its thorns, to thaw.

It took a whole day and night to defrost. A durian thawing in enclosed surroundings in the cold of winter really stinks!

It was disgusting … it really smelt like putrid, rotting flesh. It clogged up one's nostrils and hung about every nook and corner, smelling like some evil malodorous stench. I didn't dare open the windows and doors in case the smell permeated the neighbourhood and I got chased out of it. By the time it was thawed out, no one wanted to eat it anymore and I was left to consume it all by myself.

That was the only time I was disenchanted with the fruit— the smell had returned with a vengeance but was unbearably overpowering in a non-tropical environment, and the usual gorgeous flesh was one wet sloppy quivering mess. Now that is the epitome of loneliness—consuming a durian all by oneself in a foreign country when even the durian itself has abandoned you and is no longer the durian you remember.

WMD—Weapons
of Much Destruction

Coming from a country where it is a criminal offence to own a weapon, it is quite a change to be in a land where owning a gun is a common thing. In Malaysia, you could be incarcerated or even executed if you own a weapon, no matter if you have not committed murder. But in the US, one could go shopping for handguns, rifles, shotguns and semi-automatics quite easily. Approximately 40,000 gun sales, including the sale of 20,000 handgun sales, are completed every day in the US.

I was fortunate in that nothing untoward happened to me or my family during our stay there. We managed to come home to Malaysia bullet-free and unscathed, without being the focus of any loony's target practice. Of course, one can argue that the chances of getting shot at are one in a million in the US but who wants to be that one unfortunate statistic? After all, one could get blasted away just having a burger in McDonald's. It has happened before.

Day after day, one reads about senseless killings executed deliberately as well as through accidental handling of guns. In 1996, 34,040 people died from gunfire in the United States. Of these deaths, approximately fifty-four percent resulted from suicide, forty-one percent resulted from homicide and three percent were unintentional. Eight children are killed every day in the US by guns. Firearm Injuries is the eighth leading cause of death in the US. Until today, gun violence remains a very serious national problem.

What I found most chilling were the reports of young teenagers committing mass murders of their classmates and teachers. In 1998, in Jonesboro, Arkansas, two boys dressed in camouflage fatigues, waited in the woods behind their school until the lunch hour. One of them then ran into the hallway and triggered the fire alarm. As students and teachers filed out of the buildings, the two boys ruthlessly used them as target practice, opening fire on the innocent victims with high-powered rifles stolen from the grandfather of one of the boys. Four girls and an English teacher, who had attempted to shield the children from the barrage, were killed. A year later, the Columbine tragedy drew a collective gasp of horror and disbelief from the nation and the world. At the Columbine High School in Colorado, two teenage boys, loaded to the hilt with weapons, went on a rampage, shooting their teachers and schoolmates. Thirteen people died in this horrific tragedy along with the two young gunmen who finally turned their guns upon themselves.

It can be quite unnerving never knowing when one's luck has run out or if one has just stepped unknowingly on to the toes of a gun-toting wacko. If you do not go into the more unsavoury parts of the city, you are fairly safe, my American friends comfort me. I remember feeling really uneasy once when I had to stop my car at a busy intersection. I could hear the loud thumping base of a car stereo getting louder and louder. Then, a car drew up alongside mine. The driver of that car turned around and glared at me. He had a nasty and angry expression on his face. I felt trapped. I did not dare stare back. I thought to myself, "My God, what if he pulls out a gun?" I knew I was guilty of stereotyping. Perhaps he just didn't like my hairstyle. In a country where guns were available so freely, what guarantee did I have that some crazy '*tiga suku*' (Malay idiom for someone 'three-quarters' gone) would not pull out his shotgun and take a potshot at me?

Of course it is probably much easier to get killed back home in Malaysia the way we drive there. Malaysia has amongst the world's highest road fatalities. We are generally nice friendly people, who are by far too accepting of a lot of things, hoping that things will all work out for the better at the end of the day. A culture of non-confrontation permeates our everyday working lives. We are still somewhat enthralled by top-down, protocol-loaded, hierarchical structures in our society. It is no wonder then that by the time we get behind the steering wheel of a road machine that grants one anonymity but great bullying power, we become rude and inconsiderate drivers, cutting into lanes, sloughing people off roads, bearing down on hapless drivers, hogging, tailgating, maiming and taking innocent lives. Fourteen people a day die on the average. But no, we don't own guns—it's a criminal offence punishable by death to own one. But yes, we do own cars—they kill but when they do, we call it an accident.

Houston still has a raw rough edge to it. There are a number of places in Houston where my American friends warned me never to even dream of visiting or driving through.

If my car were to break down in certain parts of Houston, they warned me that I should stay inside the car. I was puzzled. It seemed like the natural thing to do to get help when one's car conks out on you.

"No. Don't even think of stepping out. Have a cell phone with you at all times so that you can call for help."

"If you don't have a cell phone, stay inside your car. Hold up a sign to ask passers-by to get help."

I realised they weren't joking when I read about the young couple who had gotten out at the wrong train station and ended up literally on the wrong side of the tracks in Flint, a town in the industrial north. They were shot dead.

One day, in Houston, a young female student from China was shot dead by a stranger in a poor part of town where she rented an apartment. She had not committed any offence. Her only 'crime' was that she looked different—an Asian who had come to live in a predominantly black and poor neighbourhood. As she did not have much money, she could not afford to live in a more upmarket area, which might have been safer for a single foreign woman.

Her parents living in China accused the US of infringing on human rights. Was it not an abuse of human rights when innocent people cannot live their lives, free of the threat of being gunned down, they demanded. Their daughter had been shot down in cold blood when walking home to her apartment. They queried how the US could preach human rights to other countries when the rights of humans in the US itself were not safeguarded? The student had left China for the US with all the good wishes and hopes of her family pinned on her. She returned dead in a box, and became yet another sad statistic.

The problem is that many Americans believe that it is the inalienable right for a person to defend himself when his or her life is in danger through the possession of firearms. This has led to a proliferation of firearms in the country and availability of guns in ordinary households. When these weapons fall into the wrong hands, they end up killing instead of defending. The other danger is accidental mishandling of guns. Just recently, a tragedy occurred when a six-year-old girl accidentally shot and killed her two-year-old brother when playing with her father's gun. One New Year's day in the US, I remember reading an incident where a Texan, in a wild celebratory mood, shot a round of bullets into the air to usher in the New Year. The bullets ricocheted and killed someone.

Do not assume though that all Americans are willing gun-toting trigger-happy citizens. There is a huge number who are anti-guns and are exceedingly unhappy at the present state of affairs. Millions are lobbying hard for stricter gun control measures and pushing for tougher laws to be introduced. One powerful movement is the Million Mom March movement. On 14 May 2000, approximately 750,000 mothers and others gathered on the National Mall in Washington, DC to demand sensible gun laws. An additional 150,000 to 200,000 people marched in support events across the country.

One can only wish them luck as they face strong opposition from politicians, right-wing Republicans, gun manufacturers, gun advocates, gun suppliers, gun dealers, the National Rifle Association, and powerful players in the arms and ammunition industry.

The US is a country that has produced many brilliant people with its tolerance and support for creativity, innovation and individualism. However, its support for individual rights has turned upon itself, forgetting that there is something called collective rights—the rights of every American (as well as resident Aliens in the US), to feel safe from gun violence. For a country founded on the rule of law, it is incomprehensible to me that something as commonsensical as stricter gun control measures and more sensible gun policies still elude the ordinary American. Or is there a more sinister reason—that the merchants of weapons of destruction want to keep it this way? In the name of human rights, of course.

Amid Treetops and Astride Camels

Coming from a small country like Malaysia and living in the US, we sometimes have to put up with really perturbing questions such as, "Do you live in trees?" Of course, don't get me wrong—not all Americans are so ignorant but there are quite a number who are still not very well-informed, I'm afraid. From a wider perspective, I guess we can't blame anyone but ourselves; for how have we impacted the world scene? What great contributions have we given to the world that the rest of it would seek us out on a map? Ahh, but we have such diverse talents and such potential … if only we Malaysians would stop obsessing about making the biggest *ketupat* (woven palm leaf pouches of pressed rice) or the fattest *roti canai* (an Indian bread) or the largest Mooncake—all of which won't exactly make the outside world sit up and figure out where we are or who we are.

During my stay in the US, I was asked at least three times about whether I and my fellow Malaysians live in trees.

The third time, I replied sweetly, "Yes, we do but nowadays we take escalators to go up the trees."

An elegant and very classy Pakistani lady I met the other day at an expat wives' Morning Coffee get-together complained that her son's American tuition teacher asked her curiously if they rode around on camels in her homeland. We all laughed, but the lady seemed terribly offended that she should ever have to straddle a camel. I told her to lighten up, after all just a few days ago, a high-powered American executive from a multinational oil company whom I was conversing with at a party, told me he had bought tonnes of toilet paper to be freighted to Malaysia, his next foreign assignment destination.

"You're kidding," I said. "But we make paper over there! What makes you think we don't have toilet paper?"

"I've never heard of Malaysia. When I got this posting, I tried to read up about Malaysia. There wasn't very much available. I am not going to take any chances. I don't mind roughing it out but I sure need toilet paper after visiting the restroom," he replied.

Well, end of conversation. I didn't want to go any further on that topic, though I was dreadfully tempted to ask him, "Whadaya think we use over there to clean our bums—leaves and *lalang*?"

Perhaps the most humorous encounter was the one that my Malay girlfriend in Houston, Soraya, related to me. Soraya was a gorgeous voluptuous lady, with thick dark brown hair, big eyes and long eyelashes—really quite a sexy-looking dame. She had just gotten married to an American called Henry. Her first husband was a very well-connected, rich and powerful Malay man, a Datuk, she told me. She had been married for many years but the marriage fell apart, and they divorced. Then she met Henry and after a brief courtship, they got married in Malaysia. They had recently relocated to the US where Henry was to take up his new post in Houston.

It was her first time in Texas. Soraya shared that she was

getting quite exasperated because she felt like an oddity. The neighbours and her husband's relatives seemed to find her unusual and were surprised that she could speak so fluently and in such beautiful English. Soraya obviously came from a wealthy and prestigious background, I could tell. She was getting fed-up with the same old questions such as:

"How come you speak such good English?"

"Did you learn English after you got married?"

"Where did you say you come from again? You must have learnt English in America."

One day, her husband's sister living in the Mid West telephones him. Henry answers the phone. Soraya overhears Henry answering questions about her, his new wife. Obviously, his sister is quite curious about her Malaysian sister-in-law and is peppering Henry with questions about her.

"Yes, Sue-Ann, Soraya's quite happily settled here in Houston. Thank you.

"No, it's not too hot for her here in Texas, Sue-Ann. It's hot in Malaysia too.

"Yes, she misses her family but she's alright.

"Er … What tribe is she from, did you say …? Er I don't know … Let me ask her … Hey Honey, what tribe are you from? My sis wants to know," asks Henry.

That did it. The wicked Soraya decided to get her own back, perhaps out of a sense of frustration at the prevailing ignorance, perhaps out of a sheer sense of mischief.

"What tribe am I from? Is that what your sister wants to know? Let me see … what tribe am I from …? Tell her … yes … tell her I'm from the Nonok tribe."

Henry obediently does as he is told.

"Hello, Sue-Ann. Soraya comes from the Nonok tribe"

"Ooohhh, the Nonoks. How interesting," is Sue-Ann's reply on the phone.

Soraya tries to stifle a smile, then starts chortling and choking, and finally collapses on the floor, almost dying of laughter.

(Only the aborigines or *orang asli* of Malaysia belong to tribes. *Nonok* is a bad word in Malay meaning a woman's private parts.)

The Red Cushion of Texas

'The Yellow Rose of Texas' was a favourite song of my parents, who enjoyed listening to the golden oldies, especially country and western music. My parents' favourite singer was Jim Reeves. 'The Yellow Rose' became one of my favourites too. Many years later, living here in Texas, I never saw any yellow roses but who can forget my Red Cushion of Texas encounter?

It happened one Sunday evening in a hot Texan summer. I was taking a walk into the housing suburb, where I lived, to pick up my son who had gone to play with his friend Jeremy. It was a pleasant housing estate of spacious homes with beautiful gardens. A typical upper-middle-class housing estate with road names such as Scarborough Fair, Manderley, Edinburgh Street and other charming Scottish and English names. I could smell the lovely scent of freshly-cut grass as proud house-owners mowed their lawns and tended lovingly to their gardens. Water sprinklers twirled drowsily in the evening sun, spraying fine mists of water on immaculate lawns.

After a short stroll, I reached Jeremy's home. I pressed the doorbell and an American woman opened the door. She was blonde with blue eyes and had the looks of a faded beauty queen.

She had big bouffant hair, and in a loud nasal voice, greeted me in a strong Texan drawl, "Oh hi there! How're ya' doin'?"

I replied in the usual Texan way, "I'm doin' fine, and how are you doin'?"

"You must be Jeremy's friend's mom! Come on in," she yelled and ushered me into her home. She was really friendly, and seemed quite excited to meet me.

"You know," she said, "you are the first Chinese I've ever met. I'm Kate."

I introduced myself. She called out to some other people in the house.

"Hey Bill, come and meet Kim."

She introduced me to her brother-in-law and Sue, another relative. They came over to where we were in the living room to say hello. Kate seemed really friendly and curious about me. She asked me some questions and from the questions she posed, I cringed inwardly and thought to myself, oh oh, it was going to be one of those days again when you wish the Americans had undergone a more comprehensive Geography curriculum in school.

"Kim, your son Jamie tells me you all are Chinese from Malaysia. Is Malaysia in China?"

I told her firstly my son's name is Jan Ming, not Jamie. And no, Malaysia is not in China, it's a country in Southeast Asia. I knew I would have to do the usual geography routine again, explaining to Americans where Malaysia is located—you know, the usual "it's-somewhere-south-of-Vietnam-and-north-of-Singapore" routine, after which you wait to see if a lightbulb switches on in the head.

"Oooh, so it's somewhere near Vietnam, I see," Kate exclaimed, but it looked quite apparent that she wasn't quite sure where Vietnam was either. "My uncle Bob served in the Vietnam War," Kate offered.

She seemed to be really excited about something. I found out in a minute or so.

"You know, Kim, I bought this red silk cushion from Neiman Marcus. It's just gorgeous! It's got this Chinese word written on it. I don't know what it means! I have been dying to find out what it means. I have asked the store people but they have no idea, and I do not know any Chinese. And here you are! Kim, you've just gotta tell me what it means. You would know!" she trilled loudly.

She went to the adjoining room—a more formal living room than the one we were in. My eyes followed her, and my heart began to sink. There, on a pristine white sofa sat this big fat red silk cushion, fashionably chinoiserie, with a single Mandarin character in bold black Chinese calligraphy.

Kate brought the cushion over, patting it fondly. "Here it is. What does it say? I'm so thrilled. I finally get to find out what it means." She fluttered her eyelashes and gazed expectantly at me.

I looked at the elegant collection of bold black strokes on the Chinese-New-Year-red cushion, with tassels on the four corners and gold braid on the edges. I had not the remotest idea what on earth it meant. I did not know the character at all though it sure looked Chinese to me. Come to think of it, no matter what letter, I wouldn't know what it meant as I didn't know any Mandarin. I only know a few phrases such as 'I love you' and 'thank you'. I probably could recognise certain characters like Chicken, Fish or Duck if I scraped the bottom of my brains. This was due to the several occasions in my life attending Chinese wedding dinners where I would scan the dinner menu, in delicious anticipation of what dishes to expect, and through the years I guess I can vaguely figure out the Chinese characters for poultry and fish.

"What does it mean, Kim? C'mon, tell us," the woman was clamouring with mounting enthusiasm. Bill and Sue were hovering politely in the background, seemingly curious too.

I never felt so put on the spot in my life. And by a cushion??! Here were these three Texans, waiting for me to unlock the linguistic secret of this fat hellish-red thing that had commanded such a presence in their living room. Here was their lucky day—a Chinese woman practically walks right into their drawing room. Here was the moment of truth … or so they thought.

Now I know what that expression 'to wish you could crawl into a hole' means … How was I going to tell Kate and her relatives I didn't have a clue! Ahh wait a minute … I do have a clue—these Mandarin characters on red cushions usually mean something like Good Luck, Longevity or Prosperity. I could say "It means Long Life" and everyone would be happy and no one would be any wiser. But I knew I couldn't do that … besides, what if they learnt the real meaning one day and it might not tally with my wild guess. Then they would have an even worse impression of us Malaysians, or Chinese.

Nope, I had to bloody own up. I had to tell them the bare shameless truth.

"Err … ummm, err … actually I'm sorry to disappoint you but I don't know what it means. Err you see, I don't know how to read Chinese," I muttered.

"WHAT??? You DON'T know Chinese! But how could that be? You ARE Chinese!" It almost sounded as if I was guilty of being born without a mother, and a tongue.

How was I going to explain to Kate and company, who

thought Malaysia was some province in China, about the complex multicultural society we Malaysians lived in, what more the other details such as the colonisation of Malaya by the British, the Chinese diaspora, the language policies in my country, the global dominance of English and the choices that we make. How was I to explain that although I didn't know Mandarin, I could speak four languages—English, Malay, Hokkien, and Cantonese. I could write in two—in English and Malay. And hey, I do understand a bit of the Baba Malay patois, although it is somewhat of a dying language. I did study Mandarin for two years in primary school and French in university, but can't remember much due to lack of practice.

I could operate with Chinese, Malays, Indians, Hispanics, Americans, Blacks, the British, the English educated, and be comfortable in all kinds of contexts be it New York or Chinatown or a *kampung* (village) in Kemaman. How do I even begin to tell Kate that it isn't a terrible shame if a Chinese cannot speak nor read Mandarin, that it doesn't make me any less Chinese, that it doesn't detract from my cultural identity anyway. That definitions of Chineseness or any kind of 'ness', for that matter, isn't such a 'pat' formula and depends a lot on one's history and circumstances.

"Ooooh you poor, POOR THING!" Kate whined, "You are Chinese and you can't read Chinese!"

Her persistence was beginning to grate on my nerves.

I looked at Kate—she had probably lived all her life in Texas. She could only speak American English and her world revolved mainly around Anglo-Americans, and probably movies from Hollywood. Relating to her all the complexities and nuances of multiculturalism and the history of another part of the world miles away would take quite some time. I tried to

explain but I felt it was too tedious for her to absorb. Besides, she wasn't interested in my history. She just wanted to know what that one blinking word on her cushion meant. Just her luck—more than one billion Chinese in the world and she had to pick me.

"I tell you what," I tried some face-saving gesture—more my face I suppose than anyone else's. "Why don't I write the word down and I will ask a friend of mine who knows Mandarin."

Kate's face burst into a happy smile.

"Wouldn't that be great! How nice of you!" she gushed.

And so, on that balmy evening in July, this Malaysian Chinese woman with four degrees in English had to do something she had never done in her life. I had to copy that one single character in Mandarin on a scrap of paper while the three Texans looked on. What a strange, messy mixture of feelings—I felt as if all the Chineseness in my blood had been drained away in that one embarrassing moment, and yet I knew deep inside, I am what I am not through any failures nor shortcomings, but merely because of historical circumstances. There was absolutely nothing to be sorry about. I didn't need to explain to death to these people as they wouldn't understand nor wanted to.

Today, if I chance to hear that beautiful lively song 'The Yellow Rose of Texas', I think of the big fat Red Cushion of Texas instead. I still don't know what that darn word means.

Alien Encounters!

My only encounters with Aliens before I went to the US was with aliens in Hollywood movies—lovable, bigheaded ones with scrawny bodies such as Steven Spielberg's *ET* or grotesque, evil, salivating creatures with multiple metallic arms such as the horrifying one in the movie *Alien* starring Sigourney Weaver, or a whole array of weird mutants in Star Wars. However, if you want to meet an Alien, and if you are not an American citizen, it's really quite easy—just go to the US and live there and you instantly qualify, for here they call foreigners Aliens.

In a sense, the US, can qualify as a Land of Aliens as it was originally a country populated by immigrants (except for the Native Americans). But over the past two to three centuries, the immigrants merged and became one country and one people, shedding their ethnic and cultural differences. And today, the visitor is branded the Alien.

Do I feel like an Alien in the US? Actually, as a Resident Alien in the US, I must say that I did come across quite a number of experiences that showed up some differences between the Texans and me.

Eye Contact Zaps

When Malaysians are in a public place, for example, in a park, and we encounter a stranger, the usual way to respect that person's privacy and to ensure one's own is to not acknowledge that person in any way—no greeting, no eye contact, not even a nod. In that way, one has not intruded into his or her private space. There is no need nor obligation to make conversation or carry on some small talk because we never got 'connected' in the first place. This, believe it or not—is respect for one's privacy. But here in the US, when two strangers meet, it is considered simple good manners to greet each other, even make some small talk. In Texas, the usual greeting is "Hi, how ya' doin'?" and you reply, "I'm good, and you?" or "Good" or something positive.

The first time I was caught in this kind of encounter was in a park in Houston. A gentleman was strolling by, and to respect his privacy, I 'graciously' ignored him. He on the other hand, was extremely uncomfortable to be in a space with another human and not establish contact. He tried to catch my eye and on finally doing so, greeted me politely. I realised then how horribly rude I must have seemed to people here when I actually was trying really hard to be polite!

After that, I willed a change in my cultural mindset and made sure I made eye contact in such encounters and greeted the person. When I returned to Malaysia, it was my turn to feel miffed at Malaysians. How come no one ever makes eye contact, why are they so rude, can't they even smile and say hello? It took some time to 'de-alienate' again.

The Great American Hug

The Chinese aren't very demonstrative in expressing love and affection in public. When we greet each other, the closest we come to human contact is the handshake. Americans are very into public demonstrations of love. Hugging and kissing is a big thing here. Hugs are hearty bearish ones. The hug is even more important than the kiss. Initially, I would freeze with anxiety when total strangers, whom I had just been introduced to came into physical contact with me so quickly, arms locking me up in a hearty hug. "Arrghhh, is he or she trying to be fresh?" Absurd thoughts would flit into my mind. Eventually, I realised that this was just a normal custom. I soon got over my cringing and it didn't take me long before I grew to appreciate the Great American Hug.

When a Malaysian friend and I take leave of each other, we would just part ways with words of farewell. But when an American friend takes leave, there is always that hug for each other. Even if there were ten friends or so, everyone would have time for a hug for each other. It made one feel special. The sense of touch is a powerful thing. After some time, when I lived in the US, I would openly hug my friends whether they were Malaysian or American. When I returned to Malaysia, it had become just a part of me to greet friends and loved ones with a big hug.

Can you imagine my surprise when upon my return I met up with my sister whom I hadn't seen for years? I had subconsciously gotten used to this American custom and gave Sis a big hug. To my astonishment, she stiffened with intense discomfort. Her body language was like, "Lay off! Eeeyahh ... don't touch me!" I got the same reaction from other close friends and relatives. An unreciprocated hug doesn't give much joy—it's like embracing a cold stiff fish in one's arms.

Back in Malaysia, I eventually learnt to regulate the right greetings and leave takings for the relevant type of friends—no hugs and kisses for my Malaysian friends who have not lived abroad, sometimes a kiss and a hug for those who have, big bear hugs for visiting American friends, and as for friends from New Zealand, Australia and Europe, that requires quite a lot of concentration to figure out how many kisses on which cheek and how often, and to hug or not to hug! Sometimes I forget what, where and who is from which country and hug my English friends American-style—and they freeze up like the Chinese, as they are NOT American!

Decibels Matter

Everything is superlatively huge in Texas. It is in fact the largest state in the US. I don't know if it is because of the large spaces involved but people speak really loudly here. I come from a culture where speaking loudly is considered aggressive and rude, so it was quite a culture shock to come across such loudness.

I remember the very first time I went shopping in a huge department store in Houston. I was browsing amidst some racks of clothing.

"HI MAM, HOW YER DOIN'? CAN I HELP YOU?" a loud nasal voice 'yelled' at me.

I jumped out of my skin, as they say. She was standing so close to me yet she was practically hollering into my ear! Did she think I was deaf?!

"Er … no thanks. I'm just browsing," I mumbled, cringing with embarrassment as I felt that everyone was looking at me. Maybe the woman thinks I am shoplifting and was checking on me under the pretext of wanting to assist me. But I found out later that this was called good service, where sales assistants come up to you and offer their services, not like back home where customer service is virtually non-existent or the salesgirl tails you around as if you were about to steal the Store Jewels.

"WELL IF YOU NEED ANYTHING, SWEETIE, JUST HOLLER, YOU HEAR ME!" she 'yelled' at me again, and strutted away.

Wowie, she called me Sweetie … I could get used to that, but holler? I'll need some practice on that as I just don't know how to holler, what more at Americans—clever people who landed the first man on the moon.

Over time, I found that in order to be heard and understood in this new vast country, I had to raise my voice by quite a number more decibels. I learnt that to be an effective communicator, being gentle and soft only ends up making you look like a ditzy bimbo. One has to hike up the assertiveness level here. No such thing as "I wonder if you could help me" if you wish to ask for something, or "Would it be possible" or "Might it be possible" and all the social niceties of the Queen's English which my mission school teachers had taught me in the good ol' school days in Malaysia.

Assertiveness mode is important here. I learnt to go straight to the point, to be direct. I learnt to say "I want you to" or "I want this" and "I want that" whenever I wanted something. Texan Americans may think that it is the most natural thing in the world to simply say what you want, but I tell ya'—it sure takes a lot of 'cultural shedding' to take on such directness after a lifetime of living in a culture where people are oblique and indirect most of the time.

Alien Senses

When you are an 'Alien', certain smells and tastes which you grew up with, and which are the most common things in the world to you, also take on an alien form in the new country which you are inhabiting. The weirdest encounter was with something as common as water. It perplexed me that no waiter nor waitress could ever understand me when I asked for water in restaurants in the US. They would bring me a glass of ice cold water with ice cubes in it, and a slice of lemon. When I tell them, "No, no, I just want warm water," they look even more perplexed than me as if they do not know what warm water is, and eventually return with a glass of boiling hot water!

"No, No. I don't want boiling hot water. I just want warm water … you know what I mean … warm water," I would plead in exasperation.

"WHAT DO YOU MEAN BY 'WARM WATER', MAM?"

"Well, er … you know, neither hot nor cold. Just warm, plain water. That's it, Plain Water! I need a glass of PLAIN water."

This would clear up the matter, I thought.

But the concept of 'Plain Water' is even more culturally alien to these Americans. I can see that they think I must have just gotten off the boat because duhhh … isn't water plain in colour and taste?

"What's with her? Does she think we are going to tinge it with ketchup or maple syrup?" I imagine they must be thinking …

I come from a culture where we drink plain, warm water all the time. Water that has been boiled then left to cool. *Air suam* the Malays call it, or *kwan suey* in Cantonese. Too much ice water is frowned upon and condemns one to possible rheumatism and arthritis in one's old age, the Chinese believe. But water at room temperature is excellent for one's health. Yet it is an alien drink here in the US, often only requested by these Aliens. I never once got my glass of warm/plain water in my entire stay in the US. It was easier to ask for boiling water and some ice cubes, and then concoct my warm water there and then.

As for smells, my favourite smells become the most foul ones over here! My two most favourite smells are the luscious smell of the durian and the simply divine smell of toasted *belachan*. To my consternation, my American friends almost faint from the 'stench' and run out of the house in agony.

Ah well, *viva la difference*. At the end of the day, I discover that the differences are but superficial ones. Our sense of proxemics, the non-verbals we employ, our haptics, oculesics, kinesics and olfactics are culture-bound, internalised by us as the result of the cultures we grew up in. I may be officially classified as an Alien but I am really not so alien after all. In the Land of the Once-These-Americans-Were-Aliens-Too, I find that we all, Resident Americans and Resident Aliens, share the same emotions, anxieties, aspirations, hopes and dreams. Aliens and Non-Aliens have similar ducts to shed our tears, the same types of facial muscles to smile or laugh, and the same organs such as hearts to soar with happiness, or break with sadness.

The Expat Wives Club

An international foreign assignment to the US sounds terribly glamorous, but for the wives accompanying their husbands, it is a mixed bag. On the one hand, there are the perks of international travel, first class air passage, limousines waiting to whisk you away to your hotel, expense accounts at luxury hotels, generous housing allowances, a free trip home every year (or the equivalent in cash), free education at expensive private schools, medical and insurance coverage, relocation expenses plus a host of other privileges.

However, the not-so-often spoken aspect of it is that the spouse has to give up her job, or put her career on hold, if she wants to accompany her partner. If you hold a high profile job or a profession, it can be quite a letdown if you find yourself sitting around in a foreign country without a job and dependent on your hubby for your survival as you no longer have the means to earn money on your own. Accompanying spouses are not allowed to work in the US, similar to the conditions imposed on spouses of expatriates in Malaysia. A lot of women who hold full-time jobs find this international posting a great break from their previous working lifestyles but there are also many who become restless and bored.

The other unglamourous side is that many accompanying spouses, previously used to the luxury of housemaids (which are common in Malaysia), end up having to tackle household chores by themselves—for some this is a first. Most Americans do not hire help and take care of the running of the household by themselves. Both partners are expected to pitch in and help in the chores, as well as the care and upbringing of the children, although statistics show that it is still the women who do the lion's share of the housework. In the US, it is largely DIY (Do-It-Yourself), when it comes to maintaining your house and doing the chores, and it is very expensive as well as uncommon to hire a live-in maid.

Thus, while expatriate wives come over to Malaysia and find, to their delight, that they can easily avail themselves to outside help such as maids, chauffeurs, gardeners if they so choose, it is quite the other way around for the poor Malaysian expat wife sent to countries like the US where she is destined to become the Minister of Home Affairs. This is fine if one is used to doing housework and thinks nothing of it, but to a certain portion of women who have never had to do housework, it is a real shock to their entire system.

To compound the problem, these women are also subjected to—not just a switch in time zones or geography—but also 'culture zones', and cultural mind sets. Many Malaysian women of a certain generation are married to men who were brought up in traditional Asian households, where the son is the little emperor, and everything is done for him from infancy to adulthood by the womenfolk. When these boys grow up and become successful professionals, don't expect them to change overnight once plonked in a foreign country. An instant cultural change of mind set? No way ... perhaps a gradual acculturation but no instant makeover after years of being feted hand and foot by Mother, Aunties, Grandmother, Wife and Maid. He just won't know how to start taking out the rubbish, like a good American husband would, nor do the laundry, iron the clothes, cook a meal, or pick up after himself overnight. You can't exactly send him to Obedience School like you could with the pet dog. You, as the non-working partner, the lady of leisure, a member of the LWL club (Ladies Who Lunch), will end up being the glorified maid—an unpaid one at that for surely, you can't charge your spouse nor his company for each hour of hard labour.

The biggest irony is if you are posted to a country like the US, there is no hardship allowance from the company. After all, you are now in the super-duper, richest and most powerful country in the world where its society prides itself on being egalitarian. No such thing as lording over other people and bossing them around, making them do menial tasks and picking up after you just because you belong to the Haves, and not the Have-Nots. But if you are from the US, and you are posted to Third World countries such as Malaysia, where one can hire two to three maids, gardener and driver, you get a hardship allowance! One really has to redefine 'hardship' here.

Most expat wives posted here to the US while away their time productively—some take up further studies or pursue postgraduate courses. Some find part-time jobs, or work voluntarily in organisations for the needy and the underprivileged. Many become actively involved in school and PTA (Parent Teacher Association) activities. Others spend their time pursuing hobbies and learning arts and crafts such as painting, pottery, embroidery, patchwork, ceramics, crochet, tapestry, or acquiring skills such as cookery, baking, photography, or learning new languages. The lifelong learning system in the US is excellent and the choices simply amazing. I enrolled for courses ranging from New Orleans Cuisine to Polynesian Dance. There are also talks on all kinds of topics such as 'The Carpets of Persia', 'Wines of Slovenia' and 'What is Chineseness?' for those who want more intellectual pursuits or just something different from the ordinary. The availability of numerous learning opportunities means that one need never be bored if one wanted something to do other than housework.

Apart from lifelong education, there is the wonderful consumerist culture—the expat wife could of course go shopping. What with the fabulous factory outlets, huge malls and stores, crafts bazaars, flea markets, one could fritter away a lot of time shopping, shopping and more shopping. With free freight provided to ferry one's things home, why worry about weight? Another favourite past time were the Morning Coffee get-togethers. Wives would gather at so-and-so's house, sip coffee, and gossip the morning away. Sometimes, a Morning Coffee was thrown to welcome a new expat wife in town or to bid farewell to someone who was going home or being relocated somewhere else. Here was the chance to show off one's house, swimming pool, dining table arrangements in the latest American fashion, one's most recent acquisitions of Noritake or Lennox or Mikasa crockery, newest silver cutlery sets, Royal Doulton fine china, or one's culinary skills, flower arrangement or table-setting skills. Some women loved playing hostess while others preferred to be invited rather than do the inviting. In the absence of jobs and professions, and with identities of Accompanying Spouses, it all depended on how each individual carved her time out here in the US—whether her life was lived meaningfully and happily, or not. Some wives were terribly unhappy, could not fit into the lifestyle here and missed the comforts of home, some could not cope—especially young mothers with large families and no support systems, some were lonely and found it hard to make new friends. On the other hand, there were those who thoroughly enjoyed the experience, forming new friendships, enjoying their travels, new cultural encounters, learning new skills. Some formed cliques and moved about like unhealthy herds of sheep following whatever the clique does or wears or eats. The stronger, more individualistic ones maintained a healthy balance of friendships for the sake of friendship and kept a wary distance from being sucked into colonies and cliques.

I had the privilege of meeting some amazing women, some of whom have become wonderful lifelong friends. But I have also met one or two unpalatable numbers—women who are envious, manipulative, who backstab and turn out to be insincere friends. Then there are those who are interested in you not as a person but in your 'potential', i.e. the position of your spouse in the company and how far/high/fast he is going up the company ladder. If he is a high flyer, chances are you're in the favoured category because you are the sleeping partner of a potential future manager, but if your spouse isn't climbing up the corporate ladder but going downhill instead, then you're not exactly top priority on the guest lists of the endless Morning Coffees or look-I'm-all-coordinated-down-to-the-place-mats dinners that some of these expat wives throw, in a mindless bid to impress.

All in all, membership in the expat wives club in the US is an enriching experience, but not as glamourous as you would like to believe it to be. I still remember the conversation I had with the wife of an American expat based in Malaysia. This took place many years ago at a Christmas party at a posh enclave in KL, long before I had set foot in the US.

She said, "You know, Kim, my life is unreal here in Malaysia. Back in the US, I was a nobody, just a nurse, just an ordinary American woman living in the Midlands of the US, really hokey-pokey country. But now here I am in Kuala Lumpur. My husband is the manager of a large multinational company here, and it's just unreal! I have an amah, maids, a driver, a gardener. I don't have to lift a finger. I live in an amazing home in Ukay Heights, and I mix with high society here, with Datuks, and Tan Sris and Y.B.s!

"And I … I play golf with royalty!" she exclaimed triumphantly.

"Then when I return to the Midlands in the US for the holidays, my boys, who have been so pampered living in Malaysia, expect me to be their amah there! They expect me to iron their clothes and do the chores. I tell them, 'Do it yourselves! I ain't your bloody amah!'"

I guess if I ever met her again, based on my recent experience as an expat wife in the US, from the Malaysian point of view, it would go something like this:

"When I lived in Malaysia, I lived like royalty. I dressed up beautifully, had my breakfast prepared by my maid, got into my car and chauffeured myself to work every day. In the evening, I would come home to a spanking-clean home, with all the ironing done, clothes neatly put away, and dinner waiting. But here in the US, I am the bloody amah!"

The Amah

It is extremely rare to have a live-in maid in the US. Not because this is not allowed, but because it is very expensive. Quite a number of expat wives I met here had been used to hiring a helper or a fulltime maid back in Malaysia. Initially, we found it tough to cope with the housework but eventually managed to adjust and get by. I had the fortune or misfortune of never having to do housework all my life until I came to the US.

From the day I was born, my family had an amah who worked for us and who became very much a part of the family. She belonged to a group of women called the black and whites, who have become extinct today. The black and white amahs came from China to Malaya in the early 20th century, seeking escape from a life of hardship and poverty for a better one overseas. In her book, *Sons of the Yellow Emperor*, Lynn Pan observes that the domestic phenomenon of amahs in East and Southeast Asia began around the 1930s when single women emigrated from Guangdong, in south China, to work as domestic servants. They became highly proficient and respected housekeepers and nannies. They were hardworking and extremely loyal. If they were happy with their employers, they would serve the family faithfully for decades, often till the end of their days.

The trademark of the amahs was the way they were dressed, in *samfoos*, consisting of a virginal white top and a pair of billowy black trousers. Amahs commonly tied their hair into a pigtail. If they had been married before, they wore their hair tied in a bun. They led simple, spartan lives and shunned materialism. They also shunned men. They were the first Chinese feminists, immigrant spinsters sworn to a life of celibacy. As unmarried women, they practised a sisterhood which celebrated their way of life. They were independent and free, and rejected the notion of having to rely on men for subsistence and livelihood.

My amah's name was Leong Yee. My parents called her Chou Chae, which means Sister Chou, while my sister, Su Win, my brother Yu Ban and I called her Chae Chae (Sister). She was a widow, and had run away from her in-laws after her husband passed away from tuberculosis. She came from a poor peasant family and was forced into an arranged marriage. On her wedding night, she was shoved into a room where her husband lay in bed, his body racking with coughs, too sick to attend his own wedding. A few months later, he died. She was blamed for bringing misfortune to the family and treated cruelly by her mother-in-law. One day, unable to bear the suffering and cruelty any longer, she decided to escape. With the help of a friend, she managed to get to a port and boarded a ship to Malaya.

She came to work in our household in 1953, and lived with us till her death in 1971. She was of stout peasant stock, with a plain looking face, big hands and big feet. She was simple and direct, honest, hardworking and a kind and lovely person at heart. She was great fun to be with, and was like a second mother to me. I remember when I scored good results in the LCE, a public examination for Form Three (Year Nine), she was overjoyed. She grabbed me by my hands, laughing with happiness and danced a little jig. Then she rewarded me by buying me a beautiful wrist watch, which must have cost a fortune to her. Although she worked as a servant, she was treated like a member of the family. She participated in all our family events and festivals, was privy to family secrets and juicy bits of gossip, mourned with the family in times of sorrow, and celebrated our moments of happiness and success.

In the absence of a family of her own, she cared for us as if we were her own loved ones. She had terms of endearments for us. She called my sister Ah Nui which means Daughter, my brother Ah Chai which means Son and she called me Mui Mui which means little Sister. We lived in an extended family with my paternal grandparents. When Grandpa fell ill, she took care of him until he passed away. She wasn't just a domestic but also a friend to the family, listening and counselling my mother, grandmother and aunts when they had problems. She was like a silent, unrecognised rock of strength—a servant in name but in reality, a strong third female presence in the household, after Grandma and Mother.

What must it have been like, on reflection, for her, coming from a culture with its overwhelming emphasis on progeny, sons and ancestor worship. No children, no descendants to pray to her memory or burn joss sticks during Ching Ming, no family except the chosen one she was working with. I do not remember a single instance of her ever wallowing in self-pity. She laughed a lot, she was a happy and carefree person with a great sense of humour. She taught us songs in Cantonese, a language we learnt from her, and she enjoyed telling us stories about her life in China. Can women totally negate or subdue their sexuality? With the amahs, it looked as if they were at peace with the choices they made in their lives, never to waver nor look back in regret.

Apart from her surrogate family here in Malaysia, she had her other family—her fellow 'sisters' in the sisterhood of the black and white amahs. The amahs devised an ingenious institution called the *kongsi*, a kind of amah sorority house. The *kongsi* was a cluster of rented rooms above a shop in Chinatown where they could spend their days off and later live permanently in retirement. They contributed regularly to the support of aged members and took care of each other. Occasionally, on her day off, Chae Chae would take my sister and I along to her *kongsi* in Petaling Street, where she would have a good yarn with her friends there while my sister and I hung around in this strange upstairs hideaway abode of spinsters only, with its steep flight of wooden stairs, austere plank floors, dark dingy rooms without beds except for foldaway mattresses, humble possessions wrapped in plastic bags stashed away in corners, the exotic smells of Chinatown wafting by.

When she was in her sixties, Chae Chae had a great yearning to return home to China again to visit her folks. She told me of her plans to visit Hong Kong with my mother, bringing along my sister and I. After Hong Kong, she planned to travel one more time to China. Her previous trip home had a tinge of sadness because she had disappointed her father deeply. She told me the story of the slippers. Her father had written to her of his great desire to own a pair of Fung Keong slippers, a popular brand in Malaysia then. On her trip home to China, she had bought a pair of slippers specially for her father. She sailed home on a P & O liner, third class, bringing with her lots of presents for her family and village folks. On her first day home, an endless stream of relatives came to visit her. Here was the prodigal daughter come home, someone who had made it overseas. They were very poor and were grateful for the presents she bought them. After they had left, it was time to give the slippers to her father. She watched as her father opened his gift excitedly, with trembling hands and much happiness all over his face. Then his expression turned to disbelief and utter disappointment. Chae Chae rushed to the old man's side and realised, to her horror, that she had not checked carefully and had brought for her father a pair of slippers, both of which were for the same left foot.

She was struck by illness before she could make her one last trip to China. She was admitted to the University Hospital and diagnosed with cancer of the womb. She passed away shortly after that. My whole family and clan mourned her passing as if she were our very own flesh and blood. She was cremated and her ashes scattered out at sea, at her request. She had fled China by boat, unwanted and unloved. In her final journey, as we travelled out to sea from Port Swettenham, and scattered her ashes into the deep blue water, much had changed—she had found a family who loved her deeply, and her passing left a void in our lives for a long time.

After Chou Chae, there were no more amahs. The phenomenon of the black and white amahs gradually became a thing of the past. The younger generation preferred to work in the factories rather than as domestics. Immigration was tightened after Malaysia's independence from the British in 1957, and women from China were no longer allowed to seek work in Malaysia.

My mother employed day helpers after that—women who dropped by and helped clean the house and do the laundry for a few hours. They came from the Shaw Road flats, in a poor gritty part of Kuala Lumpur, located across the railway track, a short distance away from where we lived.

None of them worked for very long—some were good workers but some were erratic and unreliable. I remember Panama, a poor widow whose husband had died from excessive consumption of toddy—the poor man's alcohol. She worked for us for a few years and sometimes got quite drunk herself. Once she found some turpentine in the store room and thinking that it was toddy, proceeded to down the whole bottle.

My mother's favourite was Teresa, a fat jolly Indian Catholic lady who lived in the Shaw Road flats. She could speak excellent Malay as her neighbours were predominantly Malay firefighters at the Shaw Road Fire Station. She worked with us for a long time, always jovial, with hilarious tales of the firemen and the folks who lived in her block of flats.

After I got married, I still had day help most of the time in my new home in Petaling Jaya, a suburb of Kuala Lumpur. When my son was born, we employed full-time live-in maids. First there was gentle Mila, who came to work in Malaysia when her husband lost his job in the earthquake in Baguio, then Rose, a hardworking woman whose husband had run away with her sister leaving her and her five children in the lurch. She was with us for two years of our stay in the US but then had to return home to take care of her family—her eldest daughter who had been entrusted to take care of the younger siblings, got pregnant with a seventeen-year-old schoolmate, and had to get married in a big hurry.

So, for the first time in my life, I was finally in for it here in the US—Housework! Cleaning, sweeping, mopping, dusting, washing dishes, vacuuming, cooking, ironing … I was totally in shock. Er just how does one operate a washing machine? Or a vacuum cleaner? I enjoyed the first stage tremendously—the part where I went to town and did the shopping for all the detergents I could think of which would help make my home look bright and sparkly. Shopping in American supermarkets is a wonderful experience because of the array of choices. But after that it was down to the grubby grinding mindless chores which women all over the world have to do every day but take into their stride so uncomplainingly. In this super-duper richest superpower in the world, I scored a series of Firsts—the first time I ever peered into a toilet bowl with the intention of cleaning it, the first time I cleaned one, the first time I changed bedsheets, ironed a shirt, dusted an entire house!

I learnt not to be a Martha Stewart ... no need for perfection and perfect coordination. I love cooking so preparing meals were fun. And I love water so the chores which involved playing with water was fun too. But arrghh, I hate ironing. I soon learnt to take short cuts—the clothes that needed pressing were sent to the laundry's where they would be returned two days later beautifully ironed, instead of looking as if they had survived a hurricane which was how they would appear if I ironed them. My husband was actually quite happy to pay me NOT to iron his clothes. When a hemline drooped, I whipped out my stapler and stapled the errant material back into its rightful level, as I dislike sewing and can't thread a needle for a kingdom. The support systems there are great too—the supermarkets and stores in the US are packed with homemaker-friendly, housewife-happy, prepacked, ready to roast, ready to toss, preshredded, presoaked, premarinated food items, non-crease bedsheets and wrinkle-free clothes.

At the end of the day, it really wasn't so bad after all. Being maidless—I comforted myself—means one has more privacy, more freedom and less stress having to deal with another person, although one certainly develops more calluses and coarser hands. Not to mention an eternal obsession in mopping the floor and snapping at anyone who smudged my beautifully mopped floor. I was becoming like Lady Macbeth, "Out, damn spot!" obsessed with keeping my kitchen floor clean.

This is so unreal, I thought, when in the midst of some idiotic, unintellectual household chore like cleaning the toilet bowl. Back in my homeland, a so-called 'developing' country, I spent my leisure time developing my mind, reading all sorts of books and magazines as I was spared from doing the housework. But here in the most developed country of the world, I spent so much time doing tedious humdrum household chores, developing into a cleanliness freak, fussing over the smudges and stains on my kitchen floor!

Then one lovely day in Houston, the doorbell rang. I opened the door and there was a Hispanic Mexican lady standing there, polite and demure, with soft brown eyes and wavy brown hair.

"Hola. My name is Maria. I yam looking for part-time job. Would you like to hire me?"

She was cleaning some other houses in the neighbourhood and looking for a few more to make it worth her while as she came from a long way away. Her rate was US$ 50 an hour.

Umm let me think about it ... for a few seconds ... and yes Maria, please walk right in, you are an angel sent from heaven, you are hired!

My Dog and Cat—
For Here or To Go?

It was the autumn of 1996. We were all set to leave for the US. Jimmy had left a month ahead of Jan Ming and me on an international foreign assignment to Houston, Texas. He had to start work immediately with his company in Houston as well as look for a house before the rest of the family arrived. I would take care of matters at home before joining him—sell off the cars, supervise the packing, settle any outstanding bills, switch off the electricity and gas, seal up the house, in short, tie up all the loose ends.

The company which my husband worked for flew its employees and family first class or business class to the assigned destination. Only there was a little hitch. We had two more members of the family who were not assigned free air passage. Not first nor business class, not even cargo class. Yet, to us, they were very much family. They were our pets, Ruskie our nine-year-old German Shepherd, and Patches our seven-year-old cat.

There had never been any doubts in our mind that we would bring Ruskie along wherever we might go. Jimmy and I, both animal lovers, had decided to get a dog after we got married and moved to our new home in the suburbs of Kuala Lumpur.

We bought Ruskie from a dog breeder who had advertised in the newspapers. The dog farm was located somewhere in the hills near Old Klang Road. I can still recollect walking to an enclosure where the German Shepherd puppies were kept. The owner opened the gate and out tumbled a dozen or so puppies, yapping and romping excitedly around us.

German Shepherd puppies look like adorable teddy bears with black snouts and very soft fur. One rambunctious little fellow kept frisking around us, nipping at my feet and tugging my skirt. I was about to pick him when from the corner of my eye, I saw one more puppy wobble out of the enclosure. She wore a quizzical frown, and looked rather lost. She glared at her frisky brothers and sisters, sat down on her haunches and sighed. That's the one! Both Jimmy and I fell in love with her. She was probably the runt of the litter, the weakest link but she looked so mild and gentle compared to her boisterous brothers and sisters. We picked her up and took her home.

She turned out to be a wonderful pet, loyal and intelligent beyond belief. We trained her ourselves when she was four months old. She could obey basic orders and never ever caused us any problems. She turned out to be a dear friend. She danced with us in our moments of happiness and jubilation, licked away our tears and our wounds in moments of sadness or pain. She seemed to sense every mood of ours and lived that mood along with us.

Her greatest quality was her gentleness. She was so mild of disposition that when baby Jan Ming was born, she would sit right next to the baby in his cot or stroller and my baby would be absolutely safe. Although Ruskie had been the 'baby' in our lives before our first and only child came along, there was never any question in our minds that Ruskie might get jealous or harm the new addition in our family. Indeed, she was extremely protective and knew instinctively that the baby was something very precious, and accepted the new status quo where she was now displaced in our affections.

When we had to leave for the US, we had to make a decision as to what to do with Ruskie and Patches. My sister offered to take care of Ruskie. Sis and her husband lived in a beautiful wooden house beside two streams in the forest somewhere at the foothills of the Main Range in Perak. They lived in this magical setting with a menagerie of six dogs—including two Bulls Mastiffs, a German Spitz, a Belgian Shepherd and two mongrels, two cats, five blue-eyed geese, turkeys, ducks, chickens, cockerels and a crazy monkey. Ruskie might have found the company rather diverse but I'm sure she would have loved the space. Still, we could not bear to give her up. She was part of the family. She was not an inconvenience. She would go to Texas with us.

While dogs can be very attached to their masters and mistresses, I wasn't so sure about cats. You never quite own a cat—they own you instead. If they don't like you, they will just up and leave. Patches came into our lives after we had adopted Ruskie for a year or so. Patches was a green-eyed tabby cat with a lovely coat of black, gold and white patches and a white bosom. We found her at the cattery at PAWS, a local animal shelter near the old Subang Airport. She was in a cage full of meowing felines, sitting imperiously on a piece of newspaper away from the crowd. We were taken by her delicate manners and her lovely green eyes that slanted up slightly giving her a charming oriental air. My backdoor neighbours had a quaint nickname for her—they called her Yipoon Mui (Cantonese for Japanese Girl). She was a great hunter, perennially skulking around in the garden hunting down lizards, frogs, birds, rats and coming home with strange assortments of half-eaten animal torsos and legs hanging from her mouth.

We knew we had to decide soon whether to bring Patches with us. Bringing along one pet to the other side of the world seemed rather indulgent but two was really over the top. Torn between sentiment and practicality, I did not totally shut off the option of giving up Patches for adoption. But she wasn't quite a spring chicken—she was seven years old. When we adopted her from PAWS, she was already a full grown puss. It might be easy to find takers for cute kittens, but finding a home for a middle-aged meow would certainly be a little tougher.

Three weeks before my flight to the US, my sister-in-law, Patricia, called up and informed me that her friend was willing to adopt Patches. I called Jimmy in Houston but he was adamant.

He said, "No, Kim, they come along. Both of them. They are family, we cannot desert them. We will care for them until death do us part," he said solemnly.

I was relieved, and grateful to Jimmy for his decisiveness. It would be unfair to take one and leave the other behind. Some of my friends especially the non-animal lovers thought we were crazy.

"Aiyahhh Su Kim, it's just a cat! Why not buy me a ticket instead of spending all that money on a stupid cat?" teased Fun who cannot bear anything furry that moves.

"The cats in the US are so beautiful. Why not get yourself a gorgeous Persian cat when you are there, bring it home and sell it here? Make a big profit-lah," Seow suggested, ever the business-minded one.

Another friend, Lai, tut-tutted disapprovingly, and spouted one of his Confucian-like nuggets of wisdom, "To me, a dog is a dog is a dog."

We bought two one-way tickets for Ruskie and Patches, Kuala Lumpur to Houston. The freight company taking care of them suggested we fly our pets via KLM, reputed for their excellent care in their treatment of animals. When the handlers came to collect them, I was glad we had made the decision to bring them along to the US. The moment of parting was wrenching—Ruskie panicked when we put her into her cage, crying and howling as if destined for the abattoir. Patches's cries were like something I had never heard before—bloodcurdling meows of despair. They looked at me frantically through the bars of their cages, uncomprehending, beseeching. I could only stand there and watch helplessly, relieved this separation was only temporary, and we would meet again soon in a faraway country.

They were driven to the Kuala Lumpur International Airport, and flown to the US with a stopover at Amsterdam. They were given water, fed, taken out for short walks and a stretch at the stopover. Jimmy came to meet Jan Ming and me when we arrived at the Intercontinental Airport in Houston. It was wonderful to be reunited again. Everything was so strange and unfamiliar. As he drove us to our new home, Jimmy told us with a secretive smile there was a surprise waiting for us. When we arrived, there sitting at the doorstep of our new home were our two pets! Ruskie was overjoyed to see us, wagging her tail hysterically, yelping with joy, prancing and drooling saliva everywhere, while Patches sat primly on the driveway, cool and unruffled, nonchalance personified.

We were thankful that all of us had made it safely to the US. A week later we were proven wrong. Patches fell very ill and could not eat. The vet diagnosed her as suffering from fatty liver tissue disease. Cats are territorial animals and cannot handle too much change. Once removed from their homes, they can succumb to tremendous stress and refuse to eat. The journey from Kuala Lumpur to Houston, a time span of more than 24 hours had taken its toil on her, and her liver had gotten affected.

For a month or so, she hovered near death. She could not eat at all because of liver failure. We had to force feed her through a tube implant in her throat. Fortunately, Patches still had some remaining lives left of the mythical nine lives that a cat is supposed to have. She hung on and eventually pulled through, much to the surprise of even the vet himself who thought she was done for.

Her medical bills were harrowing. While Patches recovered from liver failure, I thought I would get heart failure whenever the medical bills arrived. They were just astronomical and in US dollars, of course. While one could claim medical coverage and insurance coverage for one's children from the company, we sure couldn't do so for our pets. We had to pay up out of pocket. A smart-aleck Malaysian acquaintance suggested that we place our cat in the middle of the I-10 highway running through Houston—where the volume of traffic was so heavy, she would be run over instantly. That would be cheaper than euthanasia, she quipped. Both Jimmy and I were not very amused by that suggestion, needless to say.

Both Ruskie and Patches flourished in Texas and seemed truly happy and contented after the initial stress of global travel. Ruskie grew fatter and her fur became so fluffy she looked a size bigger. She loved going for long walks in the park. There was a big green pond where one could feed the wild ducks and geese and just watch the wonderful life revolving around the pond. Occasionally, one would stumble across a snake sunning along the footpath that meandered around this pond. Once at twilight, we saw a family of badgers trooping Indian file across the main road, disappearing into the underground drainage system. Ruskie enjoyed being the biggest creature here and loved to chase the ducks into the water or snap at their spindly feet when she thought I wasn't looking.

I met quite a number of interesting people in the park through Ruskie. Strangers would come over to admire Ruskie and pat her and strike up a conversation. Little children ran up to her and patted her lovely soft fur. Ruskie was always gentle and allowed strangers to touch her as long as she felt safe with me. I can still picture her now, her soft fur blowing in the wind, her nose twitching in excitement at the fascinating outdoor scents and the thrill of another possible chase. When spring clothed the hills in a gorgeous abundance of wild flowers and splashes of bluebonnets, I loved roaming through the hills near our home, with Ruskie by my side, ever loyal, untiringly watching over us even as she dashed about in a springtime frenzy of joy.

Ruskie never made it back to Malaysia. In the third year of our stay in Texas, Ruskie, twelve years old then, died of an illness. After a two weeks' stay at the vet's, he advised us to take her home as there was nothing he could do for her anymore. We did not have the heart to put her to sleep just yet. One night, Ruskie's condition deteriorated badly. She could not move anymore and lay on the kitchen floor helpless. But her eyes spoke a million words—they were full of fear and followed us wherever we went as if just the sight of us could help her somehow to cling on to life. I slept with her on the kitchen floor that night, stroking her all the time because it gave her comfort. She passed away peacefully that night.

In Malaysia, when our pets died, we dug a hole in the garden and buried them there. But here in Houston we could not possibly dig a grave on land that did not belong to us.

There are amazing facilities for animals in the US ranging from pet grooming salons, pet hotels, pet hospitals and even pet undertaker agencies. We decided to resort to one such undertaker company to dispose Ruskie's body.

Ruskie must be the only Malaysian dog with her ashes strewn over a piece of land near Huntersville, in Texas. The animal undertaker who came to collect Ruskie's body was very kind and understanding, behaving as if we had lost a member of the family. He gave us some time to be alone with Ruskie, then suggested we move to another room when he bundled her body away. For a certain fee, the undertakers took her corpse to be cremated and her ashes to be strewn over Texan land at a pet cemetery. Somewhere in Texas, there is a plaque with the words 'In Memory of Ruskie, From the Lee Family'. A few days later, we received sympathy cards from the vet as well as the undertaker with a photograph of the plaque erected in her memory.

Patches, however, made it back home to Malaysia when Jimmy's international assignment ended. She had grown so fat and adorable during her stay in America. She liked to stay in the house all day, curled up like a cuddly ball of fur on my sofa. She loved the weather in Texas—basking in the sunshine on warm balmy days and opting to stay inside in cooler weather. By sunset, she had booked the most comfortable place in the house, curled up in the middle of the American king-sized bed amidst the pillows, cushions and duvet. She hardly went hunting anymore as there were no lizards, rats nor birds for her to catch here. On cold winter days, when I curled up in bed to read a good book, Patches had her own ways and means to keep warm—she would jump onto the bed, settle comfortably on top of my chest facing me, and tuck her feet under her. She would gaze at me unflinchingly with her seductive green eyes, purring contentedly, until both she and I fell asleep, lending a new meaning to the phrase 'bosom pals'.

Patches returned to Malaysia, intact, healthy and alive. Because there was rabies in the US, she had to be quarantined for three weeks at the Kuala Lumpur International Airport MASkargo compound. This time she did not develop any liver problems perhaps because she had gotten used to travelling. Once home, she quickly went back to her old ways of stalking birds in the garden and going for long forays in the neighbourhood. But she always came home, stretched herself out on the softest cushions and rugs, preened herself and went to sleep.

One Sunday afternoon, three months after our return to Malaysia, Patches had just been treated to a generous portion of Kentucky Fried Chicken, her favourite. She then disappeared for a while on her usual mysterious forays. Suddenly we heard our doorbell ring and saw a neighbour standing at our gate, with Patches in his arms, lifeless. He had found her body lying on the road right in front of our home. A car had come whizzing up the road and had run over her. I took Patches from him—her body was still warm and in one piece. But she was dead.

Patches had travelled one full circle around the world, survived all sorts of mishaps and adventures. She had made it safely home, only to be killed while crossing the road. The road where we live is a straight road on a gentle incline in a quiet neighbourhood. What kind of mad driver was this to speed through a residential area? I shuddered to think what if it had been a child instead of our cat?

Jan Ming tried to rationalise Patches' death, "Mama, I think Patches used up all her nine lives. That's why she had to die."

"Yes, Jan Ming, I think her lives finally ran out," I tried to comfort him.

But I knew she hadn't run out of lives. She had just run out of luck. Just like countless thousands of Malaysians have, being killed needlessly by their very own countrymen—the inconsiderate and reckless drivers, determined to prune down the population of a country that is so blessed and relatively spared of natural disasters.

We dug a hole under the big mango tree in our backyard and buried Patches there. A tumble of beautiful furry black, gold and white into the red laterite earth, her lovely green eyes shut forever, blood stains still around her mouth.

Welcome home, Patches.

Racism and Stereotypes

"Go home to Vietnam, you rice-eating Gomer!"

A man yelled at Lim, my Malaysian friend who was travelling around Texas one summer. She was stunned. She had been living in Texas for more than fifteen years. She held a job as an adjunct professor in an American university, and she had a wonderful American boyfriend. To her, Texas was home.

"I was stunned for a moment. I just didn't know how to react. 'Go home to Vietnam'? That … that bloody fool. I've never even been to Vietnam!" she retorted, clearly still smarting from the racist slur.

"Oh, don't worry about it," I tried to soothe her.

"I know he's an illiterate roughneck. But it still hurts when you get something like that in your face," she sighed.

"And Kim, tell me, do I look Vietnamese?" she asked.

We sort of laughed about it, then dismissed it as yet another of those unfortunate encounters that one stumbles upon when in the wrong place at the wrong time.

I didn't bother to tell my friend about my first encounter with this sort of mindless racism. I remember how stunned I was, as if someone had punched me in the face or thrown a tonne of hate at me. It occurred at the most unexpected place and moment.

I was twenty-one years old and I had won a free ticket to London at a New Year's Eve Dinner and Dance. I had picked a ticket with the number 0070, playfully telling my date at the start of the evening that it was the James Bond number, and it might just get me to London. To my utter astonishment, that ticket won the grand prize in the lucky draw. It was a dream come true for I had always longed to visit England, having been so steeped in all things English throughout my academic life.

Throughout school and university, I had received an education that was on hindsight, too steeped in the traditional Western canon, and Anglo-centric in orientation. Although I was exposed to 'New Literatures in English' at university, and enjoyed authors such as V.S. Naipaul, Raja Rao, James Ngugi, Chinua Achebe, I was really comfortable with the traditional 'Greats' of English literature. I could quote stanzas from Shelley, Keats, Wordsworth and William Blake. My favourite poet was Lord Byron—beloved for his cheeky, irreverent and amorous poetry. I loved the works of Thackeray, Charles Dickens, Jane Austen and Thomas Hardy. Emily Bronte's intensely dark, Gothic novel about love, passion and denial in the Yorkshire Moors in Wuthering Heights more or less clinched it for me—I had to visit England one day.

Not surprising then that when I first arrived in England, I felt as if I was coming home ... what a strange sensation as I had absolutely no blood ties with this country except the strong ties that lured me because of the education I had received. One of my first destinations was the Lake District, a beautiful region in Cumbria in the northern part of England. This was William Wordsworth country. Wordsworth was one of my favourite

Romance poets. Quite a number of his poems were written here in the Lake District about its serenity and magical beauty. I wanted to visit the ruins of Tintern Abbey, feel the pantheistic forces of Nature which Wordsworth wrote about in his poetry, and most of all, see the hills covered by dancing daffodils "swaying and fluttering in the breeze."

I remember stepping out of the rental car on the shores of the exquisite Lake Windermere, enjoying the cool air, the peace and quiet beauty, my heart bursting with happiness. Then I saw a man standing a little distance away.

He yelled at me and my friends, "Go home, you Chinks!"

Like my friend Lim, I was stunned for a moment. It sort of paralyses you when you are caught in something that is full of inexplicable loathing. Had I been the right 'colour', would he have smiled, greeted me? Just because my eyes are a little less deep-set, more almond-shaped, my nose not as high as a Caucasian one—whatever that may mean—my complexion not one of peaches and cream but *kopi susu* (coffee with milk), I had been condemned as the Other. He had slotted me in this box in his head called 'Chinks'.

I felt like telling him, "You stupid ignoramus … I spent all my life studying and appreciating your great literary heritage and you have to spoil my one precious moment here on this most beautiful spot on Earth?"

Inside me, I am more Westernised than Sino-cised. I do not know any Chinese poet nor any Chinese author and indeed can't read Mandarin. When my son was born, I tried real hard to sing some Chinese songs to him but couldn't think of any. At the time of the Windermere incident, I had never been to China before nor had any interest in going there. My ancestors must have sailed to Malaya from China hundreds of years ago for I am sixth generation Peranakan in Malaysia. I do not feel any bonds or links to China at all, so it was rather strange being labelled a Chink.

If he had yelled, "Go home, Banana," maybe that would have been more appropriate, for I guess that's what I am, a Banana—yellow on the outside and white inside. But wait a minute—I am not yellow but Brown. I am not Chinese but Straits Chinese—a blend of Chinese and Malay, with elements from other cultures such as Javanese, Siamese, Portuguese, Dutch and English. I am not 100% white inside either—my education is just one facet of my multicultural make-up. I am melting pot and salad bowl all fused into one package tossed with a range of dressing, which I can apply depending on where I am.

Ethnic hatred and misunderstanding could be so simply eradicated if we could just travel through time a little more. It all depends on how far you want to go back in history. Take a few hundred years and you belong to this ethnic group or that group, a few more hundred years back into time and you might find that your ancestors came from the same region. Go back even further and the evidence shows we are actually from one common family thousands of years ago somewhere in Africa. It all depends on where you choose to benchmark your ethnic origin or what cut–off point you favour in the course of human evolution to determine your ethnic and cultural identity. If we all chose one same common point in time at the beginning of *Homo sapiens*, then we would all be one big family. Just blame it on the weather, religion and culture that have caused us to evolve a little different from one another. Simplistic but true, and frankly, it's tiring the way some people go on and on trying to create barriers instead of breaking them down in the light of compelling scientific evidence.

On my most recent visit to England a year ago, I was walking along a street in London when three youths walked past me. One of them caught my eye, pulled his eyes to make them slitty-looking and said, "Mushi mushi" ('hello' in Japanese) to me, grinning in a stupid way.

"Why can't these bloody racists get their facts right?" I thought to myself. I love Japanese food but I don't think I look Japanese.

I pulled my eyes into even narrower slits, bared my teeth into a rictus grin, stuck out my jaw to look like some kind of buck-toothed Charlie Chan character, and bowing gratuitously, muttered "Mushi mushi" to the young man, stereotyping his stereotyping of me.

He looked startled and backed away.

During my stay in Texas, I was fortunate in that I did not encounter too many unpleasant experiences such as what Lim experienced. Most of the time, people were really kind, polite and friendly. Sometimes, racial stereotyping did occur.

Once a conversation took place between a school clerk and I in a school office in Houston. I commented that I really missed teaching my students back home in Malaysia.

"You teach? What do you teach?" she asked, her eyebrows raised as if she hadn't heard correctly.

"I teach English in a university," I replied.

"What? You ... you teach English?!" she answered flabbergasted.

Her jaw dropped in disbelief. Somehow, it just seemed impossible for her to comprehend that non-English or non-native speakers of English could actually teach English out there in the vast beyond.

Another incident of racial stereotyping took place in my

last year in Texas, but this time it was 'positive stereotyping', if there is such a word. Angelina, an American originally from Cuba telephoned me one morning. She had to sit for her Comprehensive Exams soon at the University of Houston and she needed help as she was weak in Statistics and Mathematics. She was worried she might not be able to pass a portion of the exams which was quantitative in nature. Would I be able to give her tuition in Maths, she asked me.

"Who me?" I asked in utter surprise. Maths sure isn't one of my stronger subjects and I consider it a feat if I can get my cheque book to balance.

"I'm sorry. I can't. Why don't you ask the two doctoral students from China? They're both brilliant in Maths," I urged.

"I've tried, but they told me they've got more students than they can handle. I can pay you. I need you to teach me—just a few sessions will do."

"You've got to be joking. I am just not good in Maths," I told her.

"What?? No way. You're Chinese! All Chinese are good in Maths," she announced.

Well, thank you, I thought. After my adamant refusal, she became rather diffident towards me whenever we met at graduate school.

But hey, I'm Chinese and I'm told I'm good in Maths. That's so much better than being told to go home to China or Vietnam or Japan.

A Shopping Cart of Languages: Pushing My Trolley

Have you ever been caught in this strange dream where you think you are speaking the same language as the others but no one understands you? This happens to me sometimes in Texas. Usually in the supermarkets.

Here I am innocuously trying to buy some food in the supermarket. I come to the meat section and see some wonderful hams.

"Can I have half a pound of this ham, please?" I say to the woman behind the counter.

I get this response, "HU-UH?"

"Er … half a pound of this, please" I gesticulate and point to the delicious-looking pineapple ham.

"Oh you mean *heaff a pouun*," the woman at the meat section corrects me.

"Yes, Mam. I mean *heaff a pouun*," I submit obediently.

I eat humble pie and say *heaffapouun*. Why stick to the English I was taught in school when it doesn't work here in the US? Do as the Romans do. In my case, for the time being, do as the Texans do.

You see, Americans don't speak English. They think they

do, but they are actually speaking American. They pronounce lots of words differently from the way we learnt them in our schools which were based on the Queen's English. Or better still, it might be safer to call it British English (although the Scots, Irish and the English can't figure out each others' talk either when they speak in what they think is English). Here in America, the English is no longer what their forefathers used to speak but has evolved into a brand of its own called American English.

Quite a number of words in American English are different from British English. For instance, Americans say elevator instead of lift, gas instead of petrol, cab instead of taxi, cell phone instead of mobile phone, and spell a whole lot of words differently. But there were more new American words for me—cohort instead of batch, defreezer instead of demister, faucet instead of tap, cash deposit instead of fixed deposit, server instead of waiter, and turnpike?? What a strange word.

They—and I—were flummoxed the first time I was in a supermarket and I could not locate the trolley section. I asked several sales assistants where the trolleys were.

"Trolleys. You know, trolleys. T-r-o-l-l-e-y. The thing on four wheels you put stuff in," I explained in not-so-elegant English as I was losing my confidence over this language that I had laboured over so lovingly in schooldays, as it sure ain't working out sometimes.

"OHH, you mean the carts? The shopping carts," one sales assistant finally got what I was raving on about.

Ooops, yes, I stand corrected. "Yes, of course, the carts. Silly me. How could I not know?"

Once, someone did a Henry Higgins on me. This was at the Hong Kong supermarket in Bellaire, Houston. He wasn't a professor of languages but a Chinese butcher at the meat section of a Chinese supermarket. After I had placed an order for a pound of minced meat, he suddenly asked me, "So you-ah flomm Malaysia or Singapore-ah?"

"I'm from Malaysia. How can you tell?" I asked in surprise.

"Awww," he said, half in Cantonese and half in broken English, "People flom there speak different. They say 'minced meat'. All people flom there say 'minced meat'. Hong Kong people also say 'minced meat'. Only Americans say 'ground meat'. That how I know you flom there-loh."

"Wah, so clever-aw," I smiled at him.

He beamed. It sure gave his job a different angle—sniffing out peoples' origins behind cuts of meats, bacon, ham and chops.

"Were you educated in England?" I was asked by a Texan I met one day.

"Err ... nope. I am a homegrown product. I was educated entirely in Malaysia."

"No way. No way ... your English is far too good. You couldn't have been educated in ... er ... where's that ... Malaysia? You must have gone to school in England or something ..."

"Well, sorry to disappoint you but I went to school there and got all my degrees in English from University Malaya."

Malaysians of my generation have the advantage of having a very good command of the English language, I guess, as we went through the English medium. (The medium of instruction was English during British rule. After Malaysia got its independence in 1957, the medium of instruction was gradually reversed from English to Malay, beginning from 1970 onwards.) Still, it is disturbing to think that while one large portion of the world is using English as a second or foreign language, many in the other portion—the native speakers of English—do not seem to realise this.

The other interesting insight about my life here in Texas is that multilingualism, which is common back in Southeast Asia—especially in multicultural countries like Singapore and Malaysia—is a rare thing here. I found this out one day when I was asked how many languages I could speak in a getting-to-know-you session at a summer class at the University of Houston.

I replied, "Four languages."

I was surprised to hear a gasp from the class.

"My, you're a genius!" several students exclaimed.

I thought they were just teasing but from their looks of awe, I could tell that they were serious. This really worried me.

"Hey, please, don't get me wrong. Everybody in my country is like me. Most of us can speak more than two to three languages and dialects."

"What? What country is this?"

I was bewildered. Bilingualism and multilingualism are surely not an uncommon phenomenon. The last thing I needed in my quest here for a doctorate degree was to be regarded as a genius.

I just happened to live in Malaysia, a multicultural, multilingual country. I spoke English with my parents, learnt English and Malay in school, Cantonese from my Chinese amah and school friends, and Penang Hokkien from my mother and aunts. You need more than one language to survive in Kuala Lumpur and the rest of Malaysia.

You need Standard Malay, the official language to communicate in the civil service. You need basic Malay as well when you want to buy a packet of *nasi lemak* from the *mak cik* ('aunty'), haggle in the *pasar malam* (night market), hire a boat to go out to the idyllic islands off the east coast of Peninsular Malaysia, talk to the customs officer or plead with the policeman. You need your Chinese dialects too for how else can you order your plate of *char koay teow* or Black Hokkien Mee and give specifications like 'more *see hum*' (cockles) and '*oi chee you cha*' (want pork fat cubes).

I should have said, "Actually, I can speak six languages" as I can understand Baba Malay, and had learnt French in my university days. If you count varieties of English, I could just rake up my score to an impressive eight, as I speak Manglish and Singlish too!

Grandma used to lapse into some Hakka (a Chinese dialect) too when she was around ... I should have paid attention. That would have given me a score of nine languages then—now, if that is not Einstein, I don't know what is.

That day, I realised something quite valuable. Growing up in a multicultural country, where there is a constant barrage of diverse dialects and languages, where people codeswitch all the time, where there is such diversity of languages and cultures, I had taken it for granted. It was just a part of life. Then I came to Texas, where it is largely monolingual, and I realised that I missed all that diversity. True, there are many ethnic minorities living in Texas but the various cultures are not as integrated, and hence the localised contexts are largely monolingual in nature. Thus, to a majority of people here who only speak one language and have only one culture, someone with a command of four languages must, I suppose, appear to be hugely intelligent.

By this type of criteria then, Malaysia can now make another entry into the Malaysia Book of Records—as a nation of geniuses!

Face Off

During my first few months in Texas, I was unused to the abundance of 'sorrys' frequently being muttered. Why are people forever apologising? 'Sorry' when someone wants to cross your path, 'sorry' if someone accidentally bumps into you, 'sorry' if they can't understand you. I learnt that 'sorry' was just another way of saying 'excuse me' here. I found it quite difficult initially to switch to this way of asking to be excused. It was a culture bump for me. 'Sorry' to me meant an apology for a wrong that one has committed. It wasn't used as loosely and generally as it was here in the US.

Americans are really direct and up front. This can be so refreshing if you come from a culture where there is a lot of hedging and indirectness. However, this directness can be quite jarring sometimes especially if you're from a culture where 'face' is important. 'Face' is that intangible quality to do with our dignity, self-esteem and pride. I found this directness to be the polar opposite of the Malaysian culture, where 'face' is high priority, and if someone has a grievance with you, it is seldom spoken nor articulated.

One day, I got the brunt of this kind of up-front behaviour

in the US. The school clerk of the school where my son was enrolled got angry with me when I arrived late to pick up my child from school. It wasn't deliberate tardiness on my part. I had been caught in a horrendous traffic jam because of an accident along the notorious I-10 Highway and managed to get to the school half an hour after school had closed.

I drove into the school highway. My son skipped out from the school porch and along with him, stomped out the clerk. She had an angry look on her face.

She came right up to the driver's side, and snapped at me, "Please come on time in future to pick up your child. Don't expect us to babysit your son!"

I was stunned. Yes, I was wrong, yes, I was late. It happens sometimes, but was there a need to be so brusque? I was extremely uncomfortable with such directness. Being reprimanded in public felt as if someone had just punched me in the tummy. She had said exactly what she felt and she was right. I tried to reflect on why I was so shaken by it and realised it was a 'face' issue. She had made me lose 'face'.

She could have given me some 'face', or saved my 'face' if she had spoken in a nicer way to me, or slipped a note into my son's bag. But then, she was just being direct, something quite the norm in her culture. I, on the other hand, found that I had internalised this thing called 'face' more than I ever suspected. Back home, people will smile and be polite and then gossip, whine or complain behind your back, or worse, resort to writing anonymous poison pen letters. I learnt that a lifetime of 'face' was hard to abandon. I had never been talked to this way before in my country and found it quite a rude jolt to my system, culturally speaking.

Perhaps that is how the US achieved developed nation

status so quickly. Perhaps that is what is holding so many of us back home—this eternal confounded fear of losing face, or fear of making the other lose face, indeed fear of fear itself. Not enough people have the courage to voice their opinions or convictions. Many have been educated in systems where you never question the *cikgu* (teacher) or the person in authority. If we are forever fearful that what one says will make someone lose face, inevitably the bad sorts will get away, as no one asks questions, no one wants to query or rock the boat. 'Face' must be preserved, and soon in the name of 'face', non-accountability, non-transparency and injustices creep in.

However, the extreme end of this openness and directness of American culture was shocking and perversely titillating. Back in my society, even if your grandpa dresses in drag, and your uncle, twice removed, is a closet flasher and serial molester, and your mum has run away with the gardener, you do not wash this dirty linen in public. If possible, you hide it for as long as you can. No matter how many skeletons, stuff them into the closet and keep them there till the rattling dies down. 'What will people say? What will people say?' is the constant preoccupation for all the secrecy and semblance of morality but when asked who these 'people' are, you will get a nonplussed look. 'Face', you see, must be preserved.

Here in the US, however, everything is blabbed out in the open, in the no-holds-barred talk shows. I had never seen anything like it in my life. All the disgusting sordid details are spewed out in these talk shows in front of a life audience. Instead of announcing proudly that "My daughter has scored 13 distinctions" like the way we Malaysians like to do effusively once a year when the public exam results come out, guests on these American talks show would announce 'truths' like "My daughter is a @#$* slut!" or "My mother is a filthy bitch!". Instead of contemplating harakiri, these talk show guests would then proceed to eschew every dirty detail.

This type of television talk shows are, of course, just one type of talk show on American television. They are, for many Americans, an embarrassingly guilty pleasure, particularly because this genre has become a main provider of trash TV. The shocking revelations of promiscuity, kinkiness, infidelity, addictions, sex changes by the guests featured on the shows possess an undeniably prurient appeal amongst viewers. The show is 'chaired' by a moderator who will try and entice even more juicy and scandalous details from the guests.

These 'confessions' are abetted by a raucous audience who will shout encouragements or disparagements at them. The audience will 'eeewww', gasp, groan, jeer, clap and boo the guests. Sometimes, a member of the audience will jump to his or her feet and offer advice or chastise the guest. I watched with amazement when a mother and her daughter, both guests on one programme, accused each other of being prostitutes and nymphomaniacs, and they started slugging it out with each other. When an audience member yelled at their unseemly behaviour, they turned on her instead! On another show, an attractive and voluptuous woman confessed that she was actually a man who had undergone a sex change. The other guests who were invited on the same show were former school mates who had tormented him when he was a lanky reedy lad in school. She had connived with the TV producers to get them to appear as guests on the same show with her so that she could torment them for being so cruel to her, er … I mean him … in school, after which she proceeded to strut in front of them flaunting her figure and her newly acquired assets. The

television camera then zoomed in on each of the guest's face as the woman pranced and danced, stripper style, and wiggled her boobs at each bewildered man and sat on their laps, as the audience cheered or jeered, depending on how disgusted or how pleased they were with her style of 'revenge'.

Sometimes, the absolutely bizarre behaviour on television aroused my scepticism, and I suspect that it was put on and hyped up, anything just to get a free trip to New York or LA and to appear on television! I stopped watching these shows after a few times, because of the absolutely trashy content. But I have never forgotten that feeling of incredulity and morbid fascination when I first encountered this genre on American TV. Just who in their right minds would stoop to something so low as to assail one's family members in public and expose all the dirty details of their private lives? It was quite a change from those old Chinese kung fu movies I watched, in my teens, of men bent on revenge, intent on killing the person who had wronged his family and massacring his entire progeny if he so much as insulted his mother. I'm not sure now who is 'getting away with murder' here!

Leaving on a Jet Plane

*Go home, you must go home quickly. I cannot urge you
enough not to stay here any longer in the US. You do not
have much time.*

Go home. Go home, focus on the quality of life.

My last few days in Texas were surrealistic. It felt like I had gotten
entangled in a Hollywood movie or a TV programme, trapped in
a scene from *ER* or *General Hospital* or *Emergency* or one of those
medical dramas that are occasionally aired on the idiot box.

I was in the US again. I had accompanied my husband
to Houston in the summer of 2001 to one of the top cancer
hospitals in the world. A year after our return home to Malaysia
from the US, my husband was diagnosed with stomach cancer
and had to undergo immediate surgery in Kuala Lumpur. After
the operation, he was on the road to recovery but a few months
later, he started having digestion problems. In May 2001, he
had to go on a business trip to Houston. He was persuaded
by his company doctors to seek advice at the MD Anderson

173

Center, a top cancer treatment centre in Houston while he was there. Numerous tests were conducted on him at the centre. The endoscopy and the biopsy tests did not show any recurrence of cancer. The specialists there recommended exploratory surgery to find out why he was undergoing such rapid weight loss and reflux problems.

That morning, he had been wheeled into the surgery room for some exploratory and possible corrective surgery. I had been in the waiting room for only forty minutes when a nurse called out my name. Intuitively, I knew something had gone wrong as surgery should take at least two hours. I was ushered into a private room. I was asked to wait, the doctor would be here in a minute.

The doctor, dressed in blue overalls, appeared, looking grim. He looked like someone I had seen in a TV show, with his square jaw, his mop of tousled red hair. Through the glass window, I could see nurses, clad in light blue uniforms, busy at work, moving up and down the corridors. The door was closed. The doctor sat down on a chair a few feet away from me, sighed a long tired sigh, his shoulders drooped as if in defeat. Then, he looked at me with his piercing light blue eyes, and the grave expression on his face made my stomach contract with fear.

He opened his mouth and said something strange, "I am really sorry, but I have some very bad news. Your husband has terminal cancer."

"Term …? Terminal? What exactly do you mean by terminal?"

"The cancer has come back. It has metastasised. He has cancer of the peritoneum. He does not have much time. I am deeply sorry."

"Not much time? What do you mean by 'not much time'?" I repeated robotic-like.

The doctor sighed heavily. He looked down at the floor, unable to look at me straight in the eye, as he muttered, "Six months. He has just six months left to live."

I tried to be brave although I could feel myself falling apart from the devastating news.

"But there must be something you can do. Surely there must be some treatment. This hospital is world-renowned … surely you can do something."

The doctor put out his right hand, reached out for my left hand, and held it firmly to steady me. I can still remember that kind gesture—his fingers intertwined with mine, two strangers' hands locked in a tight grip, my knuckles clenched white in shocked reaction to the terrible prognosis, his grasp tried to convey strength and understanding in a situation that was totally incomprehensible to me, but must have occurred far too often in his job. How strange this world is, I thought … so much suffering, and yet amongst strangers, so much compassion too.

I did not realise it but my voice was breaking and I was in tears.

"He is only forty-six years old, doctor. He is far too young to die … there has got to be something that you can do …"

"I'm sorry but there is nothing. Even surgery is pointless as it will only cause more suffering. You and your husband must go home to your country soon, be with your loved ones, enjoy whatever time you have left and focus on the quality of life," the doctor advised me.

Quality of life? Why do those words crop up when death lurks around the corner? When one is alive, quality of life isn't a top priority, shoved aside for other seemingly more pressing matters, but when death hovers, quality and not quantity suddenly matters a lot.

"I cannot … I just cannot tell him this bad news. How do I tell him he is going to die?" I cringe from the horror of Jimmy being told the awful truth.

"Then I will have to tell him," the doctor assures me, "It is kinder to be cruel. Especially when the patient is young and has a family and responsibilities. You will be amazed how strong the human condition is. It is hard to take but he will be glad to know the truth. It is more cruel to give the patient hope when there isn't any."

I stayed inside the room after the doctor left, fearful to step out, unwilling to face the trauma and darkness that lay ahead. I felt caught in some nightmare. Am I not supposed to wake up here and announce triumphantly that it was all a dream? And too much television? And yet, it wasn't. This was real and it was happening, unfolding minute by minute, second by second.

A woman came into the room. She asked me if I was okay. I did not know her at all. I thought she might be a volunteer worker who counselled people in the hospital. She was slim and attractive, in her mid-thirties. She had a kind countenance and a sweet smile. She must have counselled many people, seen oceans of despair and sadness—where does she find her strength, I wondered. I poured out my heart to her. Somehow, talking to a total stranger helped. She reached out to hug me. There were tears in her eyes too as she tried to comfort me. I did not know her name but am ever grateful to her, for reminding me that wherever there is sorrow and tragedy, there is also the goodness of the human condition. Eventually, the woman left me. I sat alone in the room, still clinging to the safety of the four walls, reluctant to take that first step out to reality.

My best friend, Jeannie, rushed in. I had called her on the mobile and she had hastened to the hospital immediately. I was grateful for her friendship and her comforting presence. The next thing to do then was to go and see Jimmy—he would be coming out of the anaesthesia. I found it difficult to do so immediately. I had to collect my thoughts, summon my courage. Jeannie and I paced up and down the long corridors of the hospital aimlessly, our faces streaked with tears, stalling for time, dreading facing Jimmy with the horrible truth.

Finally we headed to the ward where Jimmy lay. He sat up in bed. He smiled slightly when he saw us, but I could tell that the doctor must have told him the terrible prognosis. His eyes were moist, but he was incredibly stoical, and put up a brave front.

In a steady voice, he looked at me, smiled weakly and said, "Kim, has the doctor talked to you? Did he tell you I have only six months left to live? My goodness, Kim, just six months."

I nod. I am a trembling shaky mess.

Then he rationalised, "Six months, six years, it doesn't matter. Time is so relative. If a person doesn't know how much time he has on earth, he might live his life aimlessly, he might live six years, ten years, and live them without any meaning. But if you know the time you have left, then you can choose how to live it. A day can be a month, a month can be a year, depending on how you live out each moment of the time you have left."

He had to stay one more night in the hospital before being discharged the next day. I stayed the night with him in the hospital room. At first we were too devastated to talk, but later we began to discuss all the things that we had to do before we left the US, the specialists and doctors to consult when we reached Kuala Lumpur, alternative therapies to try, and how to keep fighting the cancer.

Later that night, he surprised me with yet another theory,

one which I still keep to remind myself—in moments of unnecessary worry—to let go of life's petty concerns and clutter, and strive to live a more meaningful life.

He was a geologist by training. Now, he talked to me about time, not in terms of human lives but in terms of geological eras.

"A human being lives for 70 to 80 years, if lucky, up to a hundred. This seems a long time but from a geological point of view, it is nothing. We are presently living in the Quaternary Period which began less than 2 million years ago. Geological time goes back to Precambrian times, more than 550 million years ago. The Jurassic period was 200 million years ago. Humans were not even around then. Humans only existed less than 2 million years ago.

"A human being's life span then, graphically speaking, is not even a blink of an eye against the span of geological time. Yet that is all we have, all we've got. Whether I live for forty-six or sixty or a hundred years, it is inconsequential. I am just a blip in the passage of time. What is the measure of a life then? On a geological time scale, we are all nothing. We are all but tiny grains of sand in the bigger picture."

He was, as Byron puts it, "faultless to a fault." He had always been an unassuming person, and in the face of death, he was humble and did not dwell on his life's achievements, nor wallow in self pity, nor rage against the card that fate had dealt him. Some of us find some way of rationalising the twists and blows of our destiny but I was amazed that at such a harrowing time, he could argue so dispassionately about his life and his time on earth, from a geological point of view.

It was a love of nature that had brought us together in the first place. He was the young man who had courted me against a backdrop of sea, sand and stars, the shy boy whom a mutual friend had introduced to our circle of friends because of his knowledge of canoeing and rafting during our campus days. During the long vacation breaks, a group of friends got together to build a canoe and we spent many happy, idyllic times at Port Dickson, a seaside resort, riding the waves in L.C. Frank, our canoe, swimming, basking in the sun, enjoying the company of friends, singing to the strains of guitars beside blazing campfires, pondering over the state of the universe under star-studded skies.

He was the one who taught me how to recognise the constellations; the Big Dipper, the Southern Cross and Orion. The boy with the hazel brown eyes, gorgeous tanned looks and the wonderful singing voice. He captivated me with his intelligence, his gentle manners and his great knowledge of nature. A marathon runner, a long distance swimmer, a boy scout leader, a school prefect from the Victoria Institution a premier boys' school in Kuala Lumpur in his school days, and an outstanding performer in his professional career, someone who excelled in whatever he set his mind on. He excelled in his job, a high flyer because of his skills and expertise, his leadership qualities. He was a loving and devoted husband and father, and a very good friend. Yet now, his time was running out. It didn't make sense. I always thought I would be the one to go first, I was the one with the bad habits, the night owl, the one who drank too much coffee, who ate all the wonderful but not-so-healthy stuff.

"Do not grief too much," he comforted me, "Take good care of our son. I have lived a good life, been very fortunate. I have a good family, travelled all around the world, enjoyed my life, my work. I am glad to go and meet my Maker. I am tired of this sick body. I am not afraid to go."

Our last day in Texas was like our mood—dreary, grey and sad. A tornado had blown in somewhere off the coastline of Texas and brought everything to a standstill. We were thankful that the Intercontinental Airport in Houston had not been shut down. A number of friends came to see us off at the airport early in the morning. They hugged and kissed us goodbye. There was immense sadness as they knew they would never see Jimmy again. Jimmy walked out to the aeroplane with me.

We were flown out of Houston, first class on company expense. We were deeply grateful to Jimmy's American bosses— they had treated him with so much compassion and generosity, provided assistance in every way they could, and made our exit home as easy and as comfortable as possible. The vice president of his company came to visit him at his bedside in the MD Anderson Center, to bid farewell and see that everything we needed was provided for. My husband had given so much of himself, indeed his life's work to the company, it was only fitting that they did not desert him in his time of need.

The first class cabin was empty. We were the only passengers. We had the attention of the entire crew, which we did not quite relish at this awkward time. All we wanted was to be left alone to ourselves. We were pampered with impeccable service; steaming-hot fragrant towels, plush reclining seats, champagne, free flow of the finest wines, caviar, lobster, fresh flowers, great entertainment choices in the form of movies and reading material. An endless array of food was paraded in front of us, served on elegant fine bone china—from exquisitely tender Kobe Wagyu beef, lavish seafood spreads, to delicate little pastries and sumptuous desserts.

Both of us did not feel like eating. In Jimmy's case, he was having problems holding down his food and I was in no mood to dine. Jimmy told me, half-jokingly and half in earnest, that the first thing he would do when he got to heaven was to eat. The crew was remarkably professional and did not intrude or ask what was wrong with us. When we were about to leave the cabin, the chief steward pressed a bottle of champagne into my hand, wanting to compensate for the fact that we had hardly touched anything on the flight. It certainly was not due to poor service, it was because we were on another, shall I say, plane of consciousness.

After a journey of almost twenty four hours, we finally touched down at the Kuala Lumpur International Airport. Family members were there to welcome us home. It was wonderful to reconcile with our son again.

That was my last journey out of Texas.

Less than six months later, Jimmy passed away peacefully after a brave and tough battle with cancer.

Glossary

Language and Culture

Alamak—a commonly used exclamation in Malaysia. Covers an array of meanings, ranging from 'Oh my goodness!' and 'Oh dear!' to 'Help!'.

Cheongsam—a traditional Chinese one-piece dress.

Kati, tahil, gantang—old Malay units of measurement.

'La li lah tum pong'—a chant Malaysian children use to determine who will be 'It' in their game of Catch or Hide and Seek.

Lalang—a very common type of grass, thin and long with sharp edges, that grows in the wild.

Mak cik—literally Aunty, but is sometimes used as a term of respect for any female older than oneself.

Mamak—colloquialism for someone of Indian-Muslim heritage.

Manglish—Another name for Malaysian English, a variety of English used by Malaysians.

Singlish—a variety of the English language as spoken in Singapore.

Favourite Malaysian Foods

Black Hokkien Mee—a delicious noodle dish, with thick black soy sauce, stir-fried over a very hot fire.

Char koay teow—a dish made up of fried flat noodles with eggs, vegetables, seafood or chicken and pork.

Ju hu char—a Peranakan dish of julienned cuttlefish, turnip, carrots, beans and other ingredients.

Mooncakes—a Chinese confection traditionally eaten during the Mid-Autumn Festival.

Nasi—rice

Nasi lemak—rice cooked in coconut milk and usually served with anchovies, hard-boiled eggs and cucumber.

Nasi ulam—rice with herbs.

Sambal belachan—chilli prawn paste sauce, a popular accompaniment to Malay and Peranakan meals.

Teh tarik—thick, strong tea with a frothy layer. Literally means 'pulled tea'.

Top Hats—a dainty Peranakan appetiser of tiny cups made from batter, filled with shredded turnip, beans, carrots, slivers of crab meat, omelette and chilli.

Rendang, satay, popiah, mee soto, lontong, fried *mee hoon, mee siam*—popular Malaysian dishes.

Belachan cubes, *tom yam* paste, Cheong Chan soy sauce, Ghee Hiang sesame oil, *ketupat* and *rendang* mixes, *assam pedas* and *assam tumis*—a variety of sauces, mixes and bases for Malaysian cooking.